hamlyn

Baby Names & Star Signs

Robert Parry

Contents

Star signs

First published in Great Britain in 2001 by Hamlyn, a division of Octopus Publishing Group Ltd., 2–4 Heron Quays, London E14 4JP

Copyright © Octopus Publishing Group Ltd. 2001

ISBN 0 600 60319 9

A CIP catalogue for this book is available from the British Library

Printed and bound in China

10 9 8 7 6 5 4 3 2 1

Introduction

Includes useful information on the star signs, their elements,
their glyphs and advice on how to use this book.

Compatibility charts

Who gets on with whom? With the help of these charts you will see
which star signs enjoy the most harmonious relationships.

Introduction

What's in a name? Well, the answer to that question has to be, 'Quite a lot!' Our name is the only thing we wear throughout our lifetime – and yet, oddly enough, it is chosen for us by someone else. By any reckoning, that someone else is a very important person, and as a parent, or parent-to-be, that person is *you*.

So how do you go about choosing a name responsibly: one that suits your child, rather than simply reflecting your own preferences? After all, what you think is a really good name might not coincide at all with the personality of your child. Moreover, the choice is enormous, with baby-name dictionaries listing thousands of entries. What is needed is some way of narrowing down the choice to a manageable number. This book is designed to help you do just that, by providing names that match your child's astrological star sign, determined of course by his or her date of birth.

Even so, the choice is still wide enough – don't worry. Wide enough for hours, if not days, of lively discussion and argument among spouses, friends and family. In this book, however, all the names in each list have one great advantage – they suit the baby, or baby-to-be, in an astrological sense, and therefore have a good chance of being just the right apparel to wear for that lifetime to come.

What are **star signs**?

In the course of a year, the Sun appears to travel all the way around the sky in relation to the background of fixed stars. Throughout much of recorded history, the band of stars through which the Sun travels – called the zodiac – has been divided into 12 equal sections, beginning with the first day of spring (in the northern hemisphere), which in astrological lore is around 21 March each year. These sections form the star signs, 12 in all, with the Sun remaining in each one for around one month at a time as it travels through the sky.

The star signs are not all the same, but are subdivided into groups. The first subdivision is according to the four classical elements – Fire (star signs Aries, Leo and Sagittarius), Earth (Taurus, Virgo and Capricorn), Air (Gemini, Libra and Aquarius) and finally Water (Cancer, Scorpio and Pisces). Each element has its own particular characteristics:

Fire
outgoing, dynamic, inspirational

Earth
sensible, steady, dependable

Air
thoughtful, inventive, loquacious

Water
sensitive, sensual, protective

The signs are also seen as possessing qualities relating to the seasons, so we have what are called Cardinal signs at the start of each season (Aries, Cancer, Libra and Capricorn); Fixed signs in the middle of each season (Taurus, Leo, Scorpio and Aquarius); and finally Mutable (changeable) signs at the end of each season (Gemini, Virgo, Sagittarius and Pisces). Again, these divisions can be associated with certain characteristics:

Cardinal leadership, originality
Fixed loyalty, steadfastness
Mutable versatility, adaptability

Take all this together, and each sign will be different to its neighbours, with unique characteristics which over the centuries have come to be represented by symbols such as the Ram (Aries), the Bull (Taurus), and so on. These (mostly animal) representations can be seen in the glyphs for each sign, which appear throughout the book – the horns of the ram are used in the glyph for Aries, the M glyph for Virgo is the initial of Mary, the Virgin, and so on.

Of course, there is more to astrology than star signs. To determine a star sign all you need is the date of birth (see chart, opposite), which is pretty straightforward, but if you visit a properly qualified professional astrologer they will also ask you for the precise time and location of your child's birth. They will then draw up a personal birth chart – a sort of detailed map of the sky at the time and place of birth. With special attention given to the placement of the Moon and all the planets, this chart can offer all kinds of insights into the personality of an individual and the possible choices they will make in life. Nevertheless, the humble star sign remains an important factor in any appraisal of personality, and for children in particular it has always been considered significant in the early years of development.

This book deals with star signs. Each chapter is clearly structured to provide you with the information you need in order to make an informed choice of suitable names, and also offers some timely tips on how to bring up children born under each sign – for each one is unique, with different needs. When he or she grows up, your child will thank you for taking the time to 'get it right' in this way, and for your wisdom in having chosen carefully the name that best reflects his or her innermost dreams and aspirations.

♈	**Aries** The Ram	21 March to 20 April
♉	**Taurus** The Bull	21 April to 20 May
♊	**Gemini** The Twins	21 May to 20 June
♋	**Cancer** The Crab	21 June to 22 July
♌	**Leo** The Lion	23 July to 22 August
♍	**Virgo** The Virgin	23 August to 22 September
♎	**Libra** The Scales	23 September to 23 October
♏	**Scorpio** The Scorpion	24 October to 22 November
♐	**Sagittarius** The Archer	23 November to 21 December
♑	**Capricorn** The Goat	22 December to 20 January
♒	**Aquarius** The Water Carrier	21 January to 19 February
♓	**Pisces** The Fishes	20 February to 20 March

Born on the **cusp**?

If your baby was born on the cusp – that is, on the exact date on which one star sign finishes and another begins (for example 20 April, the cusp of Aries and Taurus) you should consider the subsequent sign to be of equal importance as the one that is finishing. This is because the times of the day when the Sun moves from one sign into another actually vary from year to year, and sometimes even the dates themselves are different. If you want to check up on these changes, and you have access to the internet, go to www.starnames.fsnet.co.uk, where you will find the latest changes for the year.

How **to use** this book

First of all, you need to find out which star sign your baby comes under by checking his or her birth date against the list of star signs given on page 11. Then turn to the relevant chapter, where you will find a number of different sections.

Introduction to the star sign

This section provides an overview of the basic personality of babies born under this sign, and is followed by several other useful pieces of information.

First is the ruling planet. Each sign is said to be governed by one of the planets, and these bodies, which often carry strong mythological or cultural significance, provide an important key to understanding the nature of the sign itself.

This is followed by a brief description of what the sign means in terms of its element. A baby born under a dynamic Cardinal, Fire sign, for instance, will usually be much more of a handful than, say, one born under a gentle Mutable, Water sign.

There are also notes on the physical characteristics and health of babies born under this sign, and although we now realize that these are by no means as reliable as they once seemed to our forebears, it is still interesting to consider that once upon a time each of the star signs was believed to govern a particular part of the body. For Aries it was the head; for Pisces, the feet; and so on – and strange as it may sound, these correlations are often very appropriate.

After this, we take a look at some famous people born under the sign in question, to give a flavour of how astrology works out in practice. Finally, there is a list of Lucky Connections: the traditional 'correspondences' of each sign, including gemstones, colours, plants and metals. This is vastly different to the arbitrary lists drawn up by jewellers, by the way, where each month is assigned a precious stone according to the fancy of the sales executive at the time. Rather, this is the real thing – traditional astrology, based on centuries of use. Not only are these correlations extremely helpful in understanding individual preferences, but they also provide us with a rich source list when searching for suitable names. For example, ruby is the gemstone given to Mars, the ruling planet of Aries – a splendid name to begin with!

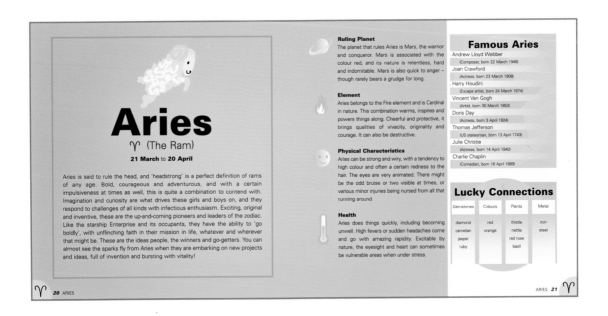

Aries
♈ (The Ram)
21 March to 20 April

Aries is said to rule the head, and 'headstrong' is a perfect definition of rams of any age. Bold, courageous and adventurous, and with a certain impulsiveness at times as well, this is quite a combination to contend with. Imagination and curiosity are what drives these girls and boys on, and they respond to challenges of all kinds with infectious enthusiasm. Exciting, original and inventive, these are the up-and-coming pioneers and leaders of the zodiac. Like the starship Enterprise and its occupants, they have the ability to 'go boldly', with unflinching faith in their mission in life, whatever and wherever that might be. These are the ideas people, the winners and go-getters. You can almost see the sparks fly from Aries when they are embarking on new projects and ideas, full of invention and bursting with vitality!

Ruling Planet
The planet that rules Aries is Mars, the warrior and conqueror. Mars is associated with the colour red, and its nature is relentless, hard and indomitable. Mars is also quick to anger – though rarely bears a grudge for long.

Element
Aries belongs to the Fire element and is Cardinal in nature. This combination warms, inspires and powers things along. Cheerful and protective, it brings qualities of vivacity, originality and courage. It can also be destructive.

Physical Characteristics
Aries can be strong and wiry, with a tendency to high colour and often a certain redness to the hair. The eyes are very animated. There might be the odd bruise or two visible at times, or various minor injuries being nursed from all that running around.

Health
Aries does things quickly, including becoming unwell. High fevers or sudden headaches come and go with amazing rapidity. Excitable by nature, the eyesight and heart can sometimes be vulnerable areas when under stress.

Famous Aries
Andrew Lloyd Webber
(Composer, born 22 March 1948)
Joan Crawford
(Actress, born 23 March 1908)
Harry Houdini
(Escape artist, born 24 March 1874)
Vincent Van Gogh
(Artist, born 30 March 1853)
Doris Day
(Actress, born 3 April 1924)
Thomas Jefferson
(US statesman, born 13 April 1743)
Julie Christie
(Actress, born 14 April 1940)
Charlie Chaplin
(Comedian, born 16 April 1889)

Lucky Connections

Gemstones	Colours	Plants	Metal
diamond	red	thistle	iron
carnelian	orange	nettle	steel
jasper		red rose	
ruby		basil	

Raising an **Aries** Child

Was that a bolt of lightning that just flashed through the room? No, it was your Aries child. These are volatile little beings who will race around recklessly and rather noisily, always on some urgent quest, getting breathless with all the excitement of life. Demonstrative, determined and fiercely independent, they insist on being in control and, with typically Arian spontaneity, are liable to throw the odd tantrum or two when crossed. And why not – they have all the bright ideas, remember? Of course they do! On the plus side, however, you will have an especially warm-hearted and affectionate child. When very young, Aries children will adore stories and games with an element of fantasy and adventure – anything that fires their imagination; when a little older, they become very sociable and outgoing, fond of sports, racing with bikes or toys, and always keen to take up challenges. Keep the first-aid box handy and be prepared for those occasional knocks and bumps as they run around endlessly chasing their dreams, or for when things don't move quite so fast as these little rams think they should – that is, instantly!

Aries in the family home

You will soon discover that Aries children are incurably adventurous. They revel in discovery and have the most vivid and lively of imaginations. By the same token, they easily become bored with having 'nothing to do' – the repeated cry of the school holidays. Affectionate and loving in their quieter moments, they become devoted to those who encourage their instincts for adventure and play. Both in and beyond the family home, Aries is what is often called a 'people's person'. Aries gets on best with their fellow fire signs, Sagittarius and Leo, though also quite well with Aquarius and Gemini.

Friendship

High-spirited and social beings, Aries children like to bounce ideas back and forth, and are usually outgoing and gregarious as a consequence. With their fondness for novelty and the Martian instinct for the rough-and-tumble of life, they will be attracted to friendships that provide the opportunity to demonstrate their powers of leadership. They have so many great plans, and others will just have to listen and take note – or else! They therefore tend to clash horns with those whose ideas are different, but will also make up quickly.

School

At school, Aries children will be fired with enthusiasm for learning new things, but might lose interest when the need for commitment takes over from the initial excitement of discovery. Don't despair! They are rarely, if ever, lazy, just easily bored, and can make up for lost time with astonishing speed whenever they suspect they might be falling behind in the race. As long as a sense of adventure in the learning process can be instilled, they become natural achievers. They excel at sports, too, and individual games like running or jumping, or anything 'martial' requiring the wielding of bats or rackets, such as cricket, baseball or tennis. They like to be winners, both on and off the field.

Hobbies and interests

Aries children are inventive and inquisitive, with a wide range of hobbies. Computers, surfing the net, sports, playing in bands, travel, collecting – everything. The typical Aries individuality and inventiveness will be applied to each of these topics in turn – or sometimes all together! Consequently, your little ram can burn through pocket money very quickly. Anything new will be an object of desire, and you will need to temper that enthusiasm sometimes just to stay solvent.

Raising your child

This section looks in detail at what parents can expect when raising their little Capricorn or Leo (or Virgo, or Aquarius …). For example, each star sign is more compatible with some signs than with others, and you'll discover this information here. (Further information on compatibility between signs is provided on pages 140–143.) Also included are special notes on family life, friendship, school and hobbies. Of course, each child is a unique individual, and may or may not fit neatly into the descriptions provided. For instance, the Piscean personality is typically placid in character, yet if your Piscean child happens to have the fiery planet Mars in conjunction with the Sun in his or her birth chart, then things are likely to be very different indeed. But these divergences are the exception rather than the rule, and are the province of detailed astrological analysis. (Further information on how you can pursue this very interesting and rewarding subject is provided on page 144.)

Choosing a name

This is the section in which we really start to analyse each sign, its ruling planet and its myriad associations in order to determine which names are suitable. The English language is a remarkably rich and fertile hunting ground, and when it comes to looking at names – even just first names, which we study here – we have to consider not only the input from the ancient Greeks and Romans and their wealth of astonishing mythology, but also the Teutonic influences from northern and central Europe. In choosing a name we can also keep one eye on the tradition of Christianity because, after all, when we name a child many of us still give to it a 'Christian name'. You will therefore find allusions here both to biblical names and to the story of Christianity itself.

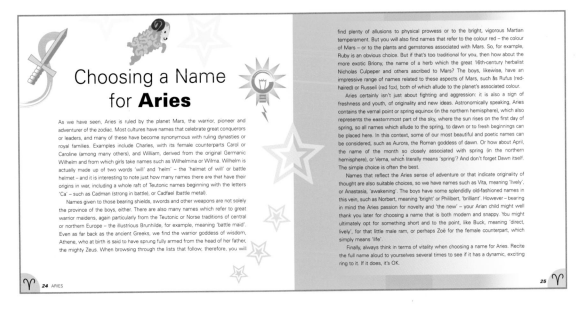

Choosing a Name for **Aries**

As we have seen, Aries is ruled by the planet Mars, the warrior, pioneer and adventurer of the zodiac. Most cultures have names that celebrate great conquerors or leaders, and many of these have become synonymous with ruling dynasties or royal families. Examples include Charles, with its female counterparts Carol or Caroline (among many others), and William, derived from the original Germanic Wilhelm and from which girls take names such as Wilhelmina or Wilma. Wilhelm is actually made up of two words 'will' and 'helm' – the 'helmet of will' or battle helmet – and it is interesting to note just how many names there are that have their origins in war, including a whole raft of Teutonic names beginning with the letters 'Ca' – such as Cadman (strong in battle), or Cadfael (battle metal).

Names given to those bearing shields, swords and other weapons are not solely the province of the boys, either. There are also many names which refer to great warrior maidens, again particularly from the Teutonic or Norse traditions of central or northern Europe – the illustrious Brunhilde, for example, meaning 'battle maid'. Even as far back as the ancient Greeks, we find the warrior goddess of wisdom, Athene, who at birth is said to have sprung fully armed from the head of her father, the mighty Zeus. When browsing through the lists that follow, therefore, you will find plenty of allusions to physical prowess or to the bright, vigorous Martian temperament. But you will also find names that refer to the colour red – the colour of Mars – or to the plants and gemstones associated with Mars. So, for example, Ruby is an obvious choice. But if that's too traditional for you, then how about the more exotic Briony, the name of a herb which the great 16th-century herbalist Nicholas Culpeper and others ascribed to Mars? The boys, likewise, have an impressive range of names related to these aspects of Mars, such as Rufus (red-haired) or Russell (red fox), both of which allude to the planet's associated colour.

Aries certainly isn't just about fighting and aggression: it is also a sign of freshness and youth, of originality and new ideas. Astronomically speaking, Aries contains the vernal point or spring equinox (in the northern hemisphere), which also represents the easternmost part of the sky, where the sun rises on the first day of spring, so all names which allude to the spring, to dawn or to fresh beginnings can be placed here. In this context, some of our most beautiful and poetic names can be considered, such as Aurora, the Roman goddess of dawn. Or how about April, the name of the month so closely associated with spring (in the northern hemisphere), or Verna, which literally means 'spring'? And don't forget Dawn itself. The simple choice is often the best.

Names that reflect the Aries sense of adventure or that indicate originality of thought are also suitable choices, so we have names such as Vita, meaning 'lively', or Anastasia, 'awakening'. The boys have some splendidly old-fashioned names in this vein, such as Norbert, meaning 'bright' or Philibert, 'brilliant'. However – bearing in mind the Aries passion for novelty and 'the new' – your Arian child might well thank you later for choosing a name that is both modern and snappy. You might ultimately opt for something short and to the point, like Buck, meaning 'direct, lively', for that little male ram, or perhaps Zoë for the female counterpart, which simply means 'life'.

Finally, always think in terms of vitality when choosing a name for Aries. Recite the full name aloud to yourselves several times to see if it has a dynamic, exciting ring to it. If it does, it's OK.

24 ARIES

25

100 names each for girls and boys

Finally, at the end of each chapter you will find the lists of names themselves. Each name has its definition set alongside it, and if you refer back to everything you have read about the particular star sign, you will discover plenty of clues as to how the connection between the name and its sign has been established. For example, under Sagittarius you will find the name Joyleen, which means 'joyful' – a clear reference to the sign's ruling planet, the expansive, jovial Jupiter. All you have to do then is choose your favourites and draw up a shortlist.

You may find the same name appearing under more than one star sign. This is because some names have qualities and meanings that are quite wide-ranging, perhaps almost universal. A good example is the name Charles, from which are derived the feminine versions Charlotte and Carla, among many others. Charles means simply 'free man' – which finds a resonance in several of the more freedom-loving and independent signs such as Aries, Gemini and Aquarius.

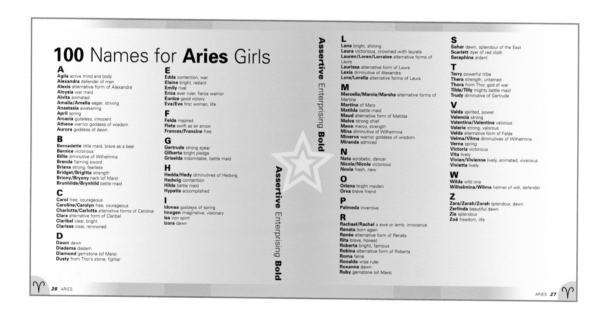

100 Names for **Aries** Girls

A
Agila active mind and body
Alexandra defender of men
Alexis alternative form of Alexandra
Aloysia war maid
Alvita animated
Amalia/Amelia eager, striving
Anastasia awakening
April spring
Arcacia guileless, innocent
Athene warrior goddess of wisdom
Aurora goddess of dawn

B
Bernadette little maid, brave as a bear
Bernice victorious
Billie diminutive of Wilhelmina
Brenda flaming sword
Briana strong, fearless
Bridget/Brigitta strength
Briony/Bryony herb (of Mars)
Brunhilde/Brynhild battle maid

C
Carol free, courageous
Caroline/Carolyn free, courageous
Charlotte/Carlotta alternative forms of Caroline
Clara alternative form of Claribel
Claribel clear, bright
Clarisse clear, renowned

D
Dawn dawn
Diadema diadem
Diamond gemstone (of Mars)
Dusty from Thor's stone, fighter

E
Edda contention, war
Elaine bright, radiant
Emily rival
Erica ever ruler, fierce warrior
Eunice good victory
Eva/Eve first woman, life

F
Felda inspired
Fleta swift as an arrow
Frances/Francine free

G
Gertrude strong spear
Gilberta bright pledge
Griselda indomitable, battle maid

H
Hedda/Hedy diminutives of Hedwig
Hedwig contention
Hilda battle maid
Hypatia accomplished

I
Idonea goddess of spring
Imogen imaginative, visionary
Isa iron spirit
Izora dawn

L
Lana bright, shining
Laura victorious, crowned with laurels
Lauren/Loren/Lorraine alternative forms of Laura
Laurissa alternative form of Laura
Lexia diminutive of Alexandra
Lora/Lorella alternative forms of Laura

M
Marcella/Marcia/Marsha alternative forms of Martina
Martina of Mars
Matilda battle maid
Maud alternative form of Matilda
Melva strong chief
Mena mercy, strength
Mina diminutive of Wilhelmina
Minerva warrior goddess of wisdom
Miranda admired

N
Nata acrobatic, dancer
Nicola/Nicole victorious
Novia fresh, new

O
Oriena bright maiden
Orva brave friend

P
Palmeda inventive

R
Rachael/Rachel a ewe or lamb, innocence
Renata born again
Renée alternative form of Renata
Rita brave, honest
Roberta bright, famous
Robina alternative form of Roberta
Roma fame
Ronalda wise ruler
Roxanna dawn
Ruby gemstone (of Mars)

S
Sahar dawn, splendour of the East
Scarlett dyer of red cloth
Seraphina ardent

T
Terry powerful tribe
Thera strength, untamed
Thora from Thor, god of war
Tilda/Tilly mighty battle maid
Trudy diminutive of Gertrude

V
Valda spirited, power
Valencia strong
Valentina/Valentine valorous
Valerie strong, valorous
Velda alternative form of Felda
Velma/Vilma diminutives of Wilhelmina
Verna spring
Victoria victorious
Vita lively
Vivian/Vivienne lively, animated, vivacious
Vivietta lively

W
Wilda wild one
Wilhelmina/Wilma helmet of will, defender

Z
Zara/Zarah/Zorah splendour, dawn
Zerlinda beautiful dawn
Zia splendour
Zoë freedom, life

Assertive Enterprising **Bold**

Assertive Enterprising **Bold**

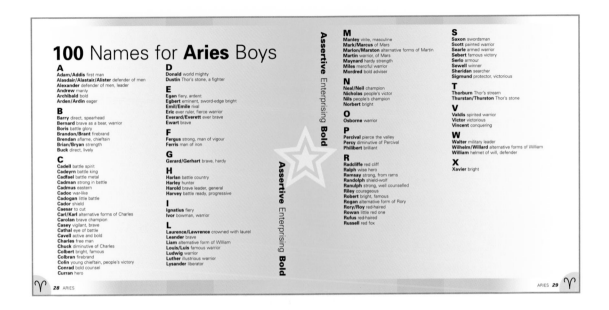

100 Names for **Aries** Boys

A
Adam/Addis first man
Alasdair/Alastair/Alister defender of men
Alexander defender of men, leader
Andrew manly
Archibald bold
Arden/Ardin eager

B
Barry direct, spearhead
Bernard brave as a bear, warrior
Boris battle glory
Brandon/Brant firebrand
Brendan aflame, chieftain
Brian/Bryan strength
Buck direct, lively

C
Cadell battle spirit
Cadeyrn battle king
Cadfael battle metal
Cadman strong in battle
Cadmus eastern
Cadoc war-like
Cadogan little battle
Cador shield
Caesar to cut
Carl/Karl alternative forms of Charles
Carolan brave champion
Casey vigilant, brave
Cathal eye of battle
Cavell active and bold
Charles free man
Chuck diminutive of Charles
Colbert bright, famous
Colbran firebrand
Colin young chieftain, people's victory
Conrad bold counsel
Curran hero

D
Donald world mighty
Dustin Thor's stone, a fighter

E
Egan fiery, ardent
Egbert eminent, sword-edge bright
Emil/Emile rival
Eric ever ruler, fierce warrior
Everard/Everett ever brave
Ewart brave

F
Fergus strong, man of vigour
Ferris man of iron

G
Gerard/Gerhart brave, hardy

H
Harlan battle country
Harley hunter
Harold brave leader, general
Harvey battle ready, progressive

I
Ignatius fiery
Ivor bowman, warrior

L
Laurence/Lawrence crowned with laurel
Leander brave
Liam alternative form of William
Louis/Luis famous warrior
Ludwig warrior
Luther illustrious warrior
Lysander liberator

M
Manley virile, masculine
Mark/Marcus of Mars
Marlon/Marston alternative forms of Martin
Martin warrior, of Mars
Maynard hardy strength
Miles merciful warrior
Mordred bold adviser

N
Neal/Neil champion
Nicholas people's victor
Nils people's champion
Norbert bright

O
Osborne warrior

P
Percival pierce the valley
Percy diminutive of Percival
Philibert brilliant

R
Radcliffe red cliff
Ralph wise hero
Ramsay strong, from rams
Randolph shield-wolf
Ranulph strong, well counselled
Riley courageous
Robert bright, famous
Rogan alternative form of Rory
Rory/Roy red-haired
Rowan little red one
Rufus red-haired
Russell red fox

S
Saxon swordsman
Scott painted warrior
Searle armed warrior
Sebert famous victory
Serlo armour
Sewell winner
Sheridan searcher
Sigmund protector, victorious

T
Thorburn Thor's stream
Thurstan/Thurston Thor's stone

V
Valdis spirited warrior
Victor victorious
Vincent conquering

W
Walter military leader
Wilhelm/Willard alternative forms of William
William helmet of will, defender

X
Xavier bright

There are also names that have more than one meaning, stemming from different cultures. For instance, Colin can mean either 'young chieftain', which puts him firmly in the Aries camp, or 'dove', which is just the opposite – a symbol of peace – and so belongs to Libra.

On the other hand, some names – often those that are the most popular, such as Paul – are not always easy to place, since Paul and its feminine equivalent Pauline simply mean 'small'. No one star sign has a monopoly on small people, you'll be glad to learn, so we have to dig a little deeper sometimes to discover the wider significance of a name of this kind. In the Bible, it was Paul who was converted to Christianity, in dramatic fashion, on the road to Damascus – so you will find Paul under Pisces, a sign often associated with faith, mysticism and philosophy. This is not to say that your little Piscean Paul might not be a giant of a baby – and if he is, and if tallness runs in the family, you might need to think again about this choice. There are plenty of alternatives to choose from and in this way you can also use the list as a filter to make sure you are not settling on a name that is blatantly unsuitable.

Say it **aloud**!

Finally, when you do settle on a name, say it aloud, together with the surname, and listen to how it all sounds. Does everything hang together? Has it got a good rhythm, or is there any odd connotation about it that could cause other children to poke fun at it? This is particularly important. Imagine yourself as a child again, standing there right in the middle of the school playground (you remember what it was like!), and call out the name in full. You may be surprised at how often you need to change things around until you end up with something that is going to be acceptable in the rough-and-tumble of the big wide world. For instance, if your family name is Burton, and you choose Kelley as a first name, the result – if you repeat it several times over – might not be too far away from Belly Button!

Make it **fun**

So there you have it. I hope you will discover from this book that names really do have amazing depth and history to them. If we didn't have names we would have to have numbers, and that would be a very dull affair. The naming of a new life, with all its boundless possibilities, has been considered a moment of great importance by people throughout history – which is why it is often accompanied by a ceremony and a celebration. And even if you don't choose your child's first name from star-sign principles, it might be a good idea at least to award him or her a second or middle name in that way. People often choose to go by their second or middle name later in life anyway, especially if they feel that the first choice is somehow not right for them.

Finally, you don't have to use these lists exclusively for naming babies. They are ideal for pets as well, or even for houses, boats or cars! For example, you may or may not feel that the name Nero (meaning 'strong and stern') is entirely appropriate for your own little Taurean child – but it might well suit a puppy born in May. In other words, have fun with this book. And if it helps to make the frantic world we live in seem a little more organized and meaningful, so much the better.

Aries

♈ (The Ram)

21 March to **20 April**

Aries is said to rule the head, and 'headstrong' is a perfect definition of rams of any age. Bold, courageous and adventurous, and with a certain impulsiveness at times as well, this is quite a combination to contend with. Imagination and curiosity are what drives these girls and boys on, and they respond to challenges of all kinds with infectious enthusiasm. Exciting, original and inventive, these are the up-and-coming pioneers and leaders of the zodiac. Like the starship Enterprise and its occupants, they have the ability to 'go boldly', with unflinching faith in their mission in life, whatever and wherever that might be. These are the ideas people, the winners and go-getters. You can almost see the sparks fly from Aries when they are embarking on new projects and ideas, full of invention and bursting with vitality!

Ruling Planet

The planet that rules Aries is Mars, the warrior and conqueror. Mars is associated with the colour red, and its nature is relentless, hard and indomitable. Mars is also quick to anger – though rarely bears a grudge for long.

Element

Aries belongs to the Fire element and is Cardinal in nature. This combination warms, inspires and powers things along. Cheerful and protective, it brings qualities of vivacity, originality and courage. It can also be destructive.

Physical Characteristics

Aries can be strong and wiry, with a tendency to high colour and often a certain redness to the hair. The eyes are very animated. There might be the odd bruise or two visible at times, or various minor injuries being nursed from all that running around.

Health

Aries does things quickly, including becoming unwell. High fevers or sudden headaches come and go with amazing rapidity. Excitable by nature, the eyesight and heart can sometimes be vulnerable areas when under stress.

Famous Aries

Andrew Lloyd Webber
(Composer, born 22 March 1948)

Joan Crawford
(Actress, born 23 March 1908)

Harry Houdini
(Escape artist, born 24 March 1874)

Vincent Van Gogh
(Artist, born 30 March 1853)

Doris Day
(Actress, born 3 April 1924)

Thomas Jefferson
(US statesman, born 13 April 1743)

Julie Christie
(Actress, born 14 April 1940)

Charlie Chaplin
(Comedian, born 16 April 1889)

Lucky Connections

Gemstones	Colours	Plants	Metal
diamond	red	thistle	iron
carnelian	orange	nettle	steel
jasper		red rose	
ruby		basil	

Raising an **Aries** Child

Was that a bolt of lightning that just flashed through the room? No, it was your Aries child. These are volatile little beings who will race around recklessly and rather noisily, always on some urgent quest, getting breathless with all the excitement of life. Demonstrative, determined and fiercely independent, they insist on being in control and, with typically Arian spontaneity, are liable to throw the odd tantrum or two when crossed. And why not – they have all the bright ideas, remember? Of course they do! On the plus side, however, you will have an especially warm-hearted and affectionate child. When very young, Aries children will adore stories and games with an element of fantasy and adventure – anything that fires their imagination; when a little older, they become very sociable and outgoing, fond of sports, racing with bikes or toys, and always keen to take up challenges. Keep the first-aid box handy and be prepared for those occasional knocks and bumps as they run around endlessly chasing their dreams, or for when things don't move quite so fast as these little rams think they should – that is, instantly!

Aries in the family home

You will soon discover that Aries children are incurably adventurous. They revel in discovery and have the most vivid and lively of imaginations. By the same token, they easily become bored with having 'nothing to do' – the repeated cry of the school holidays. Affectionate and loving in their quieter moments, they become devoted to those who encourage their instincts for adventure and play. Both in and beyond the family home, Aries is what is often called a 'people's person'. Aries gets on best with their fellow fire signs, Sagittarius and Leo, though also quite well with Aquarius and Gemini.

Friendship

High-spirited and social beings, Aries children like to bounce ideas back and forth, and are usually outgoing and gregarious as a consequence. With their fondness for novelty and the Martian instinct for the rough-and-tumble of life, they will be attracted to friendships that provide the opportunity to demonstrate their powers of leadership. They have so many great plans, and others will just have to listen and take note – or else! They therefore tend to clash horns with those whose ideas are different, but will also make up quickly.

School

At school, Aries children will be fired with enthusiasm for learning new things, but might lose interest when the need for commitment takes over from the initial excitement of discovery. Don't despair! They are rarely, if ever, lazy, just easily bored, and can make up for lost time with astonishing speed whenever they suspect they might be falling behind in the race. As long as a sense of adventure in the learning process can be instilled, they become natural achievers. They excel at sports, too, and individual games like running or jumping, or anything 'martial' requiring the wielding of bats or rackets, such as cricket, baseball or tennis. They like to be winners, both on and off the field.

Hobbies and interests

Aries children are inventive and inquisitive, with a wide range of hobbies. Computers, surfing the net, sports, playing in bands, travel, collecting – everything. The typical Aries individuality and inventiveness will be applied to each of these topics in turn – or sometimes all together! Consequently, your little ram can burn through pocket money very quickly. Anything new will be an object of desire, and you will need to temper that enthusiasm sometimes just to stay solvent.

Choosing a Name
for **Aries**

As we have seen, Aries is ruled by the planet Mars, the warrior, pioneer and adventurer of the zodiac. Most cultures have names that celebrate great conquerors or leaders, and many of these have become synonymous with ruling dynasties or royal families. Examples include Charles, with its female counterparts Carol or Caroline (among many others), and William, derived from the original Germanic Wilhelm and from which girls take names such as Wilhelmina or Wilma. Wilhelm is actually made up of two words 'will' and 'helm' – the 'helmet of will' or battle helmet – and it is interesting to note just how many names there are that have their origins in war, including a whole raft of Teutonic names beginning with the letters 'Ca' – such as Cadman (strong in battle), or Cadfael (battle metal).

Names given to those bearing shields, swords and other weapons are not solely the province of the boys, either. There are also many names which refer to great warrior maidens, again particularly from the Teutonic or Norse traditions of central or northern Europe – the illustrious Brunhilde, for example, meaning 'battle maid'. Even as far back as the ancient Greeks, we find the warrior goddess of wisdom, Athene, who at birth is said to have sprung fully armed from the head of her father, the mighty Zeus. When browsing through the lists that follow, therefore, you will

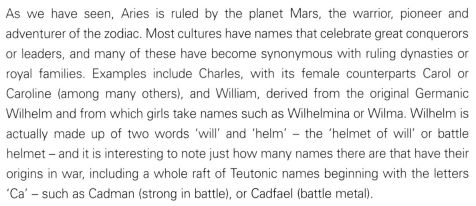

find plenty of allusions to physical prowess or to the bright, vigorous Martian temperament. But you will also find names that refer to the colour red – the colour of Mars – or to the plants and gemstones associated with Mars. So, for example, Ruby is an obvious choice. But if that's too traditional for you, then how about the more exotic Briony, the name of a herb which the great 16th-century herbalist Nicholas Culpeper and others ascribed to Mars? The boys, likewise, have an impressive range of names related to these aspects of Mars, such as Rufus (red-haired) or Russell (red fox), both of which allude to the planet's associated colour.

Aries certainly isn't just about fighting and aggression: it is also a sign of freshness and youth, of originality and new ideas. Astronomically speaking, Aries contains the vernal point or spring equinox (in the northern hemisphere), which also represents the easternmost part of the sky, where the sun rises on the first day of spring, so all names which allude to the spring, to dawn or to fresh beginnings can be placed here. In this context, some of our most beautiful and poetic names can be considered, such as Aurora, the Roman goddess of dawn. Or how about April, the name of the month so closely associated with spring (in the northern hemisphere), or Verna, which literally means 'spring'? And don't forget Dawn itself. The simple choice is often the best.

Names that reflect the Aries sense of adventure or that indicate originality of thought are also suitable choices, so we have names such as Vita, meaning 'lively', or Anastasia, 'awakening'. The boys have some splendidly old-fashioned names in this vein, such as Norbert, meaning 'bright' or Philibert, 'brilliant'. However – bearing in mind the Aries passion for novelty and 'the new' – your Arian child might well thank you later for choosing a name that is both modern and snappy. You might ultimately opt for something short and to the point, like Buck, meaning 'direct, lively', for that little male ram, or perhaps Zoë for the female counterpart, which simply means 'life'.

Finally, always think in terms of vitality when choosing a name for Aries. Recite the full name aloud to yourselves several times to see if it has a dynamic, exciting ring to it. If it does, it's OK.

100 Names for **Aries** Girls

A

Agila active mind and body
Alexandra defender of men
Alexis alternative form of Alexandra
Aloysia war maid
Alvita animated
Amalia/Amelia eager, striving
Anastasia awakening
April spring
Arcacia guileless, innocent
Athene warrior goddess of wisdom
Aurora goddess of dawn

B

Bernadette little maid, brave as a bear
Bernice victorious
Billie diminutive of Wilhelmina
Brenda flaming sword
Briana strong, fearless
Bridget/Brigitta strength
Briony/Bryony herb (of Mars)
Brunhilde/Brynhild battle maid

C

Carol free, courageous
Caroline/Carolyn free, courageous
Charlotte/Carlotta alternative forms of Caroline
Clara alternative form of Claribel
Claribel clear, bright
Clarisse clear, renowned

D

Dawn dawn
Diadema diadem
Diamond gemstone (of Mars)
Dusty from Thor's stone, fighter

E

Edda contention, war
Elaine bright, radiant
Emily rival
Erica ever ruler, fierce warrior
Eunice good victory
Eva/Eve first woman, life

F

Felda inspired
Fleta swift as an arrow
Frances/Francine free

G

Gertrude strong spear
Gilberta bright pledge
Griselda indomitable, battle maid

H

Hedda/Hedy diminutives of Hedwig
Hedwig contention
Hilda battle maid
Hypatia accomplished

I

Idonea goddess of spring
Imogen imaginative, visionary
Isa iron spirit
Izora dawn

Assertive Enterprising **Bold**

L

Lana bright, shining
Laura victorious, crowned with laurels
Lauren/Loren/Lorraine alternative forms of Laura
Laurissa alternative form of Laura
Lexia diminutive of Alexandra
Lora/Lorella alternative forms of Laura

M

Marcella/Marcia/Marsha alternative forms of Martina
Martina of Mars
Matilda battle maid
Maud alternative form of Matilda
Melva strong chief
Mena mercy, strength
Mina diminutive of Wilhelmina
Minerva warrior goddess of wisdom
Miranda admired

N

Nata acrobatic, dancer
Nicola/Nicole victorious
Novia fresh, new

O

Orlena bright maiden
Orva brave friend

P

Palmeda inventive

R

Rachael/Rachel a ewe or lamb, innocence
Renata born again
Renée alternative form of Renata
Rita brave, honest
Roberta bright, famous
Robina alternative form of Roberta
Roma fame
Ronalda wise ruler
Roxanna dawn
Ruby gemstone (of Mars)

S

Sahar dawn, splendour of the East
Scarlett dyer of red cloth
Seraphina ardent

T

Terry powerful tribe
Thera strength, untamed
Thora from Thor, god of war
Tilda/Tilly mighty battle maid
Trudy diminutive of Gertrude

V

Valda spirited, power
Valencia strong
Valentina/Valentine valorous
Valerie strong, valorous
Velda alternative form of Felda
Velma/Vilma diminutives of Wilhelmina
Verna spring
Victoria victorious
Vita lively
Vivian/Vivienne lively, animated, vivacious
Vivietta lively

W

Wilda wild one
Wilhelmina/Wilma helmet of will, defender

Z

Zara/Zarah/Zorah splendour, dawn
Zerlinda beautiful dawn
Zia splendour
Zoë freedom, life

100 Names for **Aries** Boys

A

Adam/Addis first man
Alasdair/Alastair/Alister defender of men
Alexander defender of men, leader
Andrew manly
Archibald bold
Arden/Ardin eager

B

Barry direct, spearhead
Bernard brave as a bear, warrior
Boris battle glory
Brandon/Brant firebrand
Brendan aflame, chieftain
Brian/Bryan strength
Buck direct, lively

C

Cadell battle spirit
Cadeyrn battle king
Cadfael battle metal
Cadman strong in battle
Cadmus eastern
Cadoc war-like
Cadogan little battle
Cador shield
Caesar to cut
Carl/Karl alternative forms of Charles
Carolan brave champion
Casey vigilant, brave
Cathal eye of battle
Cavell active and bold
Charles free man
Chuck diminutive of Charles
Colbert bright, famous
Colbran firebrand
Colin young chieftain, people's victory
Conrad bold counsel
Curran hero

D

Donald world mighty
Dustin Thor's stone, a fighter

E

Egan fiery, ardent
Egbert eminent, sword-edge bright
Emil/Emile rival
Eric ever ruler, fierce warrior
Everard/Everett ever brave
Ewart brave

F

Fergus strong, man of vigour
Ferris man of iron

G

Gerard/Gerhart brave, hardy

H

Harlan battle country
Harley hunter
Harold brave leader, general
Harvey battle ready, progressive

I

Ignatius fiery
Ivor bowman, warrior

L

Laurence/Lawrence crowned with laurel
Leander brave
Liam alternative form of William
Louis/Luis famous warrior
Ludwig warrior
Luther illustrious warrior
Lysander liberator

M
Manley virile, masculine
Mark/Marcus of Mars
Marlon/Marston alternative forms of Martin
Martin warrior, of Mars
Maynard hardy strength
Miles merciful warrior
Mordred bold adviser

N
Neal/Neil champion
Nicholas people's victor
Nils people's champion
Norbert bright

O
Osborne warrior

P
Percival pierce the valley
Percy diminutive of Percival
Philibert brilliant

R
Radcliffe red cliff
Ralph wise hero
Ramsay strong, from rams
Randolph shield-wolf
Ranulph strong, well counselled
Riley courageous
Robert bright, famous
Rogan alternative form of Rory
Rory/Roy red-haired
Rowan little red one
Rufus red-haired
Russell red fox

S
Saxon swordsman
Scott painted warrior
Searle armed warrior
Sebert famous victory
Serlo armour
Sewell winner
Sheridan searcher
Sigmund protector, victorious

T
Thorburn Thor's stream
Thurstan/Thurston Thor's stone

V
Valdis spirited warrior
Victor victorious
Vincent conquering

W
Walter military leader
Wilhelm/Willard alternative forms of William
William helmet of will, defender

X
Xavier bright

Taurus

♉ (The Bull)

21 April to 20 May

Being a bull may sound fiercesome, but most of the time Taurus is one of the sweetest, most placid individuals you could ever hope to meet. This tranquil nature accompanies a love of pleasure, beauty, the arts, the countryside, good living and fine foods. Expect therefore a steady, capable, loving and industrious youngster – most of the time. The exceptions are when Taurus children are teased or coerced: they will then dig in their heels, immovable like the bull itself. Remember, too, that the bull can also charge when angered. This is a rare occurrence, and in practice the odd blunt rebuttal is all that will arise. But beware: it really can be a case of the 'bull in a china shop' if genuinely angered. Meanwhile, the prudent ways of Taurus children are evident in their handling of financial affairs. They can become great savers and shrewd investors.

Ruling Planet

Venus, the planet of harmony and romance, rules Taurus. Associated with the qualities of proportion and beauty, the fruitful and productive Venus brings an appreciation of the finer things in life, and relates to money and possessions as well. Venus is also a peacemaker. It strives for balance in all things.

Element

Taurus is a Fixed, Earth sign – hence the notorious Taurean obstinacy when crossed. These are solid, dependable individuals, sometimes a little 'stodgy', though deeply sensuous as well and 'earthy' in humour. In fact, they have a natural affinity with the earth, the source of one of their great loves: food.

Physical Characteristics

Look out for a certain thick-set build. The boys will be physically strong, with thick 'bovine' necks. The girls are usually very feminine. They love fine clothes and usually dress well.

Health

Being generally placid and gentle beings, Taurus children rarely seem to suffer from stress-related illnesses. They can fall prey to laziness, however, leading to obesity or poor circulation. The throat, ruled by Taurus, is often a delicate area as well.

Famous Taureans

Yehudi Menuhin
(Violinist and conductor, born 22 April 1916)

Barbra Streisand
(Actress and singer, born 24 April 1942)

Michelle Pfeiffer
(Actress, born 29 April 1957)

Audrey Hepburn
(Actress, born 4 May 1929)

Sigmund Freud
(Psychoanalyst, born 6 May 1856)

David Attenborough
(Television wildlife presenter, born 8 May 1926)

Fred Astaire
(Actor and dancer, born 10 May 1899)

Margot Fonteyn
(Ballerina, born 18 May 1919)

Lucky Connections

Gemstones	Colours	Plants	Metal
sapphire	sky blue	columbine	copper
lapis lazuli	green	primrose	
coral	turquoise	violet	
	pastels	sorrel	

Raising a **Taurus** Child

Perhaps more than any other sign, Taurus responds to kindness and love, and this is an important key to understanding the psyche of the bull. Forget all about angry bulls: Taureans are almost always just the opposite of angry, and because of this they like their surroundings to reflect peace and harmony. Both girls and boys will want their creature comforts in abundance, and the girls in particular will be fond of beautiful things about the home – pleasant colours, fragrances and sounds. The boys, meanwhile, will have hearty appetites and will enjoy the security and warmth of family meals taken together around the table. When they are a bit older, expect those little bulls to start venturing outside, enjoying the garden or walks with the family. In fact, being a very strong Earth sign, Taurus has a natural affinity with the great outdoors as well as enjoying the home. Farms, gardens, animals, even field sports might well be a draw – and might surprise you by appearing relatively high up on the wish list for holiday ideas.

Taurus in the family home

Taurus children will soak up the traditional comfort and cosiness of home life, delighting in gentle sounds, soft colours and cuddly toys. They like people who are peaceful and calm, and especially their easy-going Earth-sign counterparts Virgo and Capricorn, though they also get on quite well with Pisces and Cancer. And, because it means security, they are at their happiest when their surroundings display a certain opulence and comfort. However, if teased or bullied in any way, or if they suspect they are being treated unjustly, little bulls can become very obstinate and stubborn indeed. It is then almost impossible to get them to budge. Appeal to their warm, loving natures if you wish to break the deadlock. Kindness and a simple cuddle will work wonders.

Friendship

Taurus children prize friendship highly and enjoy the company of those with similar temperaments to themselves: that is, reasonable, gentle, affectionate souls rather than loud, aggressive children. They may sometimes play boisterously – but never, or very rarely, with malice or aggression. They will enjoy the school disco, making music and entertaining others at home, and if you can lay on a good spread for all those hungry visitors, so much the better. Taureans become fashion conscious at a remarkably early age, and will team up with those interested in popular music, fashion and dance.

School

With their steady, methodical approach, Taurus children make excellent students. Moreover, if the connection between study and the building of a comfortable and prosperous lifestyle can be established at an early age, it will focus their Taurean minds marvellously, and possibly drive them on to great achievement. If this is lacking, then a certain laziness is always a danger.

Hobbies and interests

Taurus children have a natural flair for colour, design, fashion, music, dance and drama. Let them have access to musical instruments, paints and crayons, which they will adore. Taureans also love food, especially sweet things, and they can become comfort eaters. On the plus side, they enjoy fresh air, gardens and things that grow, and because they also enjoy financial security and saving, a piggy bank would be a prize possession for any Taurus child. Who knows, you might have a real financial whizz-kid on your hands!

Choosing a Name
for **Taurus**

Colourful, cheerful and sensuous, the month of May is celebrated in the northern hemisphere for its joyful energy and dazzling beauty. Moreover, this wonderful time of the year echoes the essential Taurean nature very closely – namely the love of all things natural, of being close to the earth and all its treasures. In this respect, the girls have the advantage in those exclusively feminine names of the months – April and May.

In many ancient cultures, springtime was celebrated by images of floral goddesses, who took their names from the word 'flower' or 'flower maiden' – a source, therefore, of delightful names such as Floris or Florence, and more subtle variations like Chloris, meaning 'blooming, fresh', or Anthea, 'lady of flowers'. Chloë is a popular modern name, but it too comes from ancient times and means 'blooming, green shoots'. Then there are the jewel names belonging to Taurus, which include Sapphire and Coral – all of which seems to leave the boys somewhat short-changed. However, characteristics of the bovine species such as strength, masculine self-confidence and robust determination can all be brought to bear in choosing a name for the Taurus male – from the conservative Desmond, meaning 'man of the world', to the more unusual Ethan, meaning 'firmness'. Names that refer to the Taurean qualities of thrift or financial acumen can also be employed in naming the little bull, including Spencer, meaning 'provider, dispenser of riches' – indicative of the safe, dependable nature of the Taurus male.

The ruling planet of Taurus, Venus, provides us with plenty more correlations and suggestions for names. Venus, goddess of love in Roman mythology, is still called the 'morning star' or 'evening star' (depending on its position relative to the Sun). Apart from the Sun and Moon, Venus can become the brightest object in the sky at such times and was considered to be a powerful force in the ancient cultures of Assyria and Babylon. Apart from the obvious choice of the name Venus itself for a girl, there are many others with the same meaning, such as Danica, Ishtar, Estelle and, in Welsh, Gwendydd. Venus, or her Greek predecessor Aphrodite, was born from the sea, and so there has always been an association between the ocean and Taurus. So Coral, 'from the sea', is a name which can be considered as well.

Love and romance aside, Venus and Taurus are both associated with many of the good things in life, and draw heavily on the qualities of harmony, proportion and beauty. This can lead to a love of well-appointed houses and equally splendid gardens full of fresh flowers, fragrances and colour to delight the eye and adorn the home. In this context there are names such as Harriet, 'mistress of the home', or Adelaide, 'of noble estate', from which comes the derivative Heidi (originally from the Germanic Adalheit).

But it is when we consider the deep Taurean connections to the Earth element that some of the most powerful names arise. Great earth goddesses of antiquity such as Rhea, Erda and Gaia provide still more possibilities for the girls, while for the boys we can draw upon the ever-popular George, 'farmer', or Henry, 'ruler of the home'. Then there is the more unusual Denham or Denman – names meaning 'from the valley'. The boys can also take names that resonate with the strong, supportive qualities of Earth, such as Piers – which comes from Peter, both meaning 'rock' and both just perfect for that legendary Taurean dependability and steadfastness.

100 Names for **Taurus** Girls

A

Adelaide/Adele of noble estate
Alcyone calm
Alda rich
Amanda lovable
Amanta loving
Anthea lady of flowers
Aphrodite goddess of love (Venus)
April month (partly of Taurus)
Aveline alternative form of Evelyn
Azura blue

B

Bela God's earth
Bethany house of figs
Beverley from the beaver's meadow

C

Chloë blooming, green shoots
Chloris blooming, fresh
Colleen girl
Columbine flower (of Venus), dove
Constance/Connie steadfast, faithful
Coral from the sea
Cottina crown of wild flowers

D

Daisy/Daisie/Dasie herb/flower (of Venus)
Dakapaki blossom
Damaris gentle
Danica morning star
Deborah bee-like, sweet, diligent
Desirée desired
Duretta little steadfast one

E

Edith happy, cheerful
Edlyn rich, gentlewoman
Edna pleasure
Elvetta wise home-ruler
Erda earth goddess, worldly
Erianthe sweetness, many flowers
Estelle/Esther morning star (Venus)
Evelyn/Eveline pleasant
Ezara little treasure

F

Fae she who trusts
Fidelia faithful
Fidonia thrifty
Fleur/Flur/Fflur flower
Flora goddess of flowers
Floranthe blossom
Florence blooming
Florentina/Florinda flowery
Floris flower-like

G

Gaia earth goddess
Garlanda adorned with flowers
Gemma jewels
Georgia/Georgina farmer
Glendora gift of the glen
Gwendydd morning star

H

Hameline home lover
Harmonia harmony, unity
Harriet/Hattie mistress of the home
Haru spring
Heidi diminutive of Adelaide
Henrietta ruler of the home
Hestia goddess of the hearth

Firm Artistic **Patient**

I

Imelda moderate
Inga/Ingrid fair, fertile
Irene messenger of peace
Ishtar earlier (Assyrian) Venus

K

Kalma calm
Kuni country born

M

Mae/May month (partly of Taurus)
Mayna home woman
Miriam strong, fertile, wished-for child
Moira gentle

N

Nerine sea born (Venus)
Nydia home-maker

O

Odette prosperity
Olive/Olivia peace
Owissa bluebird, of spring

P

Pacifica peaceful
Patience calm, endurance
Petra rock, reliable
Phillis/Phyllis leafy
Philomena love and strength
Primalia spring-like
Primavera fragrant promise, spring
Primrose flower (of Venus)
Prudence careful, prudent
Prunella plant (of Venus)

R

Rebecca peacemaker, beauty
Rhea earth goddess

S

Sapphire gemstone (of Venus)
Serena calm, serene
Shirleen sweet
Sorrel herb (of Venus)

T

Tansy herb (of Venus)
Tara hill, earth goddess
Terrena earthly pleasure
Thalia to bloom

V

Valma/Valmai May flower
Vanessa butterfly
Venus planet ruling Taurus
Vesta goddess of the hearth
Viola/Violante alternative forms of Violet
Violet/Violetta violet, modesty

Z

Zadie affluent

100 Names for **Taurus** Boys

A

Abelard noble firmness
Adonis of manly beauty
Ainsley one meadow, his own self
Alan/Allan/Allen/Alun concord, rock
Aylsworth of great wealth
Aymon ruler of the home
Azal the mountain's foundation

B

Bailey enclosure
Balfour pasture
Barton farmer
Beltane May-day
Bentley from the winding meadow
Benton from the meadow
Blair field
Bradley dweller in the broad meadow

C

Caspar treasurer
Columba/Columbia dove
Constantine faithful, resolute
Courtenay/Courtney dweller at the farm
Cowan stone mason
Craig rock

D

Dale dweller in the valley
Dalton dweller in the vale
Darius wealthy, preserver
Denham from the home in the valley
Denman from the valley
Desmond man of the world
Durand enduring, lasting

E

Eberard hardy, strong
Edmund alternative form of Edward
Edward guardian of property
Enan anvil, firm
Ethan firmness
Ezar treasure

F

Fabian grower of beans
Ferdinand peace, readiness
Fidel faithful
Florean/Florian floral beauty

G

Garth enclosure
Gentilis of kindness
George farmer
Gerius steadfast
Glen/Glenn from the glen
Godfrey peace of god
Goodard resolute, pious
Gordon great hill, spacious fort
Gorham dweller at the mud house
Gorman of clay
Grasham/Gresham dweller on the grassland

Firm Artistic **Patient**

H

Hadley landowner
Hamlyn home-lover
Hamo/Haymo home
Hanley of the meadow
Harding resolute, strong friend
Hardwin alternative form of Harding
Hartman firm
Havilah plentiful treasure
Hector holding fast, firm
Hedley upper meadow
Heinrich alternative form of Henry
Henley home-lover
Henry ruler of the home
Hew/Hugh/Hugo mindful, thinker
Howard worker with a hoe, farmer
Hume home-lover
Humphrey/Humphry supporting peace, home protector

J

Jasper treasurer
Jefferson son of peace
Jeffrey/Geoffrey peaceful ruler

K

Kelby from a farm
Kendale chief of the dale

L

Landor country dweller
Langley dweller at the long meadow
Lea/Lee sheltered, meadow
Leland from meadows

M

Malcolm devotee of the dove
Manfred man of peace
Maynard might, hardy

N

Nero strong, stern

O

Ortensio gardener

P

Paine of the country
Parker keeper of the estate
Peter rock, reliable
Piers alternative form of Peter

S

Selwyn prosperous
Sholto sower
Silvanus god of farming
Sofian devoted
Solomon peace, wisdom
Spencer provider, dispenser of riches
Stacy stable, reliable
Stewart/Stuart steward

T

Trevor great homestead, discreet

U

Unni modest

W

Wade meadow
Warren park, keeper
Wayne wagon, cartwright
Westley west meadow
Winston friend's farm, stone

Y

Yardley dweller in pasture

Z

Zurial god is my rock

Gemini

♊ (The Twins)

21 May to **20 June**

Alert, witty, dynamic, elusive – these are just a fraction of the terms that can be applied to the versatile Gemini personality. Geminis are always on the move, mentally quick and very inquisitive. There is always something to say, something new to investigate, something new to ask – so parents need to be ready with plenty of answers, and a good supply of energy to keep up. Words come naturally to Geminis, as do writing, and solving puzzles and riddles. The head is a place where they spend much of their lives. Geminis are also famed for being able to do more than one thing at a time – in fact, usually several. They often seem to be in more than one place at the same time, as well! Sociability, loquacity and self-expression go hand in hand with occasionally less appealing traits such as exaggeration, indifference to the feelings of others and even a little cunning in order to get their own way.

Ruling Planet

Gemini is ruled by Mercury, and the term 'mercurial' is very apt. Mercury is also a metal, though one which is liquid in its normal state, being slippery and malleable. In Gemini, these qualities bring great versatility and adaptability. Mercury also has a connection to medicine and communication.

Element

Air is the element belonging to Gemini, which is also classed as a Mutable sign. Air is the medium of communication: our vocal cords use air, and modern communications technology travels through the air, of course. Gemini is one of the great communicators of the zodiac.

Physical Characteristics

Geminis tend either to be tall or to present a typically compact and sprightly figure – mercurial, short, powerful and busy, gesticulating with hands and arms.

Health

Gemini rules the arms and hands, as well as speech and the vocal cords. Illnesses brought on by stress or repetitive strain are possibilities, as are respiratory complaints. Health issues are important for Gemini, and some interest in or involvement with the healing arts is common.

Famous Gemini

Bob Dylan
(Singer and poet, born 24 May 1941)

Vincent Price
(Actor, born 27 May 1911)

Isadora Duncan
(Dancer, born 27 May 1878)

Kylie Minogue
(Singer, born 28 May 1968)

Bob Hope
(Comedian, born 29 May 1903)

J.F. Kennedy
(US President, born 29 May 1917)

Venus Williams
(Tennis player, born 17 June 1980)

Sir Paul McCartney
(Singer, musician and composer, born 18 June 1942)

Lucky Connections

Gemstones	Colours	Plants	Metal
beryl	white	iris	mercury
crystal	yellow	elderflower	(quicksilver)
agate	patterns	hazel	
		myrtle	

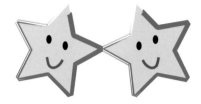

Raising a **Gemini** Child

Even if you only have one Gemini child to bring up, you will probably feel you have at least two on your hands most of the time. These mercurial little beings are here, there and everywhere, wanting to explore, full of curiosity and questions. It is vital to provide freedom and opportunities for stimulation and learning for their versatile personalities, because their horizons are broad and their minds will be turning over rapidly with ideas and observations. Expect an interest in communications and transport, in stories of all kinds and even a little local journalism at a very early age – anything, in fact, that stretches their powers of observation and enables them to move around from place to place. These are the great impersonators, the smooth operators, the entertainers and entrepreneurs of the zodiac. In Gemini you have the future businessmen and women, the wheelers and dealers with dazzling skills of communication and anticipation. Don't worry about providing lengthy explanations – with their lightning brain-power, Gemini children probably know what you are about to say even before you do!

Geminis in the family home

For Geminis, home is a base for exploration, not a place in which to mooch about. They may not be the tidiest of children, either. Toys will be taken apart to see what makes them tick, leaving long trails of various bits and pieces around the home. The personal space of a typical Gemini is a bit like Noah's Ark, moreover, with everything coming in twos. Expect Gemini children to have two hamsters or two computers in their room, or even to have two sets of their favourite toys or dolls. The girls will be as practical as the boys. Geminis usually get on well with their siblings – the more the merrier – and best of all with fellow Air signs Libra and Aquarius, though also quite well with two of the Fire signs, Aries and Leo.

Friendship

Geminis enjoy the company of people who can help them socialize and communicate their ideas and observations, so outings of all kinds will be popular. If not actually physically expressed, this search for stimulation and interaction with others could be diverted inwards – into computers and cyberspace, surfing the Internet – and they might need help in striking a healthy balance.

School

Fast learners, little Geminis will want to read early on and will be brilliant at expressing ideas in language – any language you choose, in fact. They will be good mimics, sharp in any argument. The Mutable nature of the sign means that Geminis are more likely to follow than lead, but this does not stop them analysing things and drawing their own conclusions. Subjects that challenge the brain might be favoured more than sports, so a good, rational explanation of the virtues of fitness might be necessary from time to time.

Hobbies and interests

Geminis have numerous hobbies, often several on the go at once and none of them pursued to any depth, until one day, at last, that single all-consuming passion takes over. This will be an intense affair (lasting all of five minutes) – then off they go again! Expect changes, different directions, different topics, all churning around in that over-active Gemini brain. That's why computers are a heaven-sent invention for Geminis They love them! They are also pretty clever with anything requiring dexterity or working with their hands, and may have a fondness for medicine or the healing arts.

Choosing a Name
for **Gemini**

With its ruling planet Mercury, the winged messenger of the gods, Gemini is often associated with the ideas of communication, messages and messengers. Angels and other winged spirits are very prevalent notions in ancient cultures as well as more contemporary religions, and – true or false – they even find a resonance in today's technologically driven age in the guise of aliens, the elusive and shining occupants of UFOs. This could be a good starting point in your search for a suitable Gemini name – even though you might not think of your little one as an angel just yet – with something like Angela for a girl or Michael, the archangel, for a boy. There are many less familiar (and less angelic) alternatives, however. Possibilities include Amos, meaning 'messenger of God', and Iris, the name of the bearer of messages between the gods of Olympus and the earth. Iris travelled so often between the two worlds that she availed herself of the rainbow bridge that led from one to the other. This concept echoes well the variegated, multi-coloured preferences of Gemini.

Messengers also include symbolic creatures such as birds, notably the dove, symbol of peace. There are many names in ancient cultures that refer to doves, and here Gemini must share several names with its neighbour, Taurus, peace being a quality much loved by that sign, too. Calum, meaning 'dove', or Chenoa, 'white dove' are possible name choices. In classical art, meanwhile, Mercury is usually depicted as wearing winged sandals or a winged helmet, making him every bit a creature of the air, so that many other bird names – such as the chattering Jay, for instance – make excellent choices for the nimble, eloquent Gemini personality.

According to the great 16th-century herbalist Nicholas Culpeper, the plants of Gemini include hazel and myrtle, both of which are girls' names, of course. The clever, swift-footed nature of Gemini also finds a suitable resonance in those figures of folklore that we call elves or sprites, and it is surprising just how many names there are that refer to the 'little people': Elva, meaning 'elfin'; Elladora, the 'gift of the elves'; and many more are included in the accompanying lists.

Names that suggest freedom and independence must appear here as well, because Gemini is nothing if not a free thinker. So the traditional Charles or Charlotte, or the pairing of Frances and Francis, each meaning 'free man' or 'a traveller from France', are all excellent choices.

Returning to the element of Air, from the earliest times the winds were considered to have magical properties, bringing with them all the miraculous changes of the seasons. The element of Air that Gemini typifies naturally calls upon names such as Keith, meaning 'wind', or the more exotic Nodin or Notus, with similar meanings.

In mythology, Mercury with his famous staff, the caduceus entwined with serpents, has always been strongly related to medicine, so names suggesting the healing arts can be employed in this context, such as Jason, 'healer'. Also anything referring to 'light', specifically the enlightenment of the mind, must feature in any list of names for this most intellectual and thoughtful of signs. So too with the word 'white', or anything that refers to brightness or bright waves – such as Guinevere, meaning 'white wave', from which we derive our modern-day Jennifer or Jenny. Meanwhile, boys can take the flattering Dexter, meaning 'skilful', or the unusual Alber, 'agile mind' – both ideal for those little doctors-to-be.

100 Names for **Gemini** Girls

A

Adione traveller's friend
Agnola angel
Althea to heal
Amelia industrious
Angel/Angela/Angelica angelic
Aniela angel
Awel breeze

B

Beryl multicoloured gemstone (of Mercury)
Bianca fair
Blanche white

C

Caileigh/Caleigh alternative forms of Kailey
Callena talkative
Carla/Carly/Charlie alternative forms of Carol
Carol/Carole alternative forms of Caroline
Caroline/Carolina free
Carrie alternative form of Caroline
Catalina small parrot
Celesta/Celestine heavenly
Centella flashing light
Charlene/Charleen/Sharleen alternative forms of Carol
Charlotte alternative form of Caroline
Chenoa white dove
Cholena bird
Clairine bright maid
Clara/Clare bright, clear
Claresta bright glory
Clarette little bright one
Claribel alternative form of Clara
Clarissa alternative form of Clara
Colinette little dove
Columbe/Columbia dove
Concetta ingenious idea

D

Dallas playful, skilful
Delphinia loving sister
Devnet white wave
Diaphenia transmitting light
Digna worthy
Docila/Docilla willing to learn
Donalda little mistress
Donella little damsel
Dova dove
Dromicia swift

E

Eereena messenger of peace
Elberta nobly bright
Eldora gift of wisdom
Elera elfin wisdom
Elgiva gift of the elves, clever
Ellien light
Elva elfin
Elvia of keen mind
Elvina wise and friendly
Elwyn white-browed
Erlina little elf
Erlinda lively
Eulalia of fair speech

F

Fenella white-shouldered
Finna white
Fleta swift as an arrow
Frances free, from France

Versatile Spontaneous **Active**

G

Gabriella/Gabrielle/Gaby after archangel Gabriel
Goewin/Goewyn sprightly
Guinevere white wave
Gwynne white, blessed

H

Hazel tree (of Mercury)
Hermione from Hermes (Mercury)
Hilary cheerful
Hohoka wild dove
Huga diminutive of Huguette
Huguette intellectual

I

Idelle clever, happy
Iris messenger goddess of the rainbow
Ismena learned one

J

Jemima dove
Jennifer alternative form of Guinevere
Jenny diminutive of Jennifer
June month (partly of Gemini)
Juniata ever-youthful maid
Junilla alternative form of Juniata
Juventia goddess of youth

K

Kailey/Kaylee/Kayley slender, fair
Kalya healthy
Kathini little bird
Kayleah/Kayleen alternative forms of Kailey
Keshena swift in flight
Kina/Kineta active, messenger

L

Lalla/Lallie/Lally diminutives of Eulalia
Linette song bird

M

Mahala sweet singer
Marella of bright intellect
Mavis song thrush
Mededa chatterer
Melika lyrical
Michaela/Mikaela archangel
Millicent/Millie industrious
Myrtle herb/flower (of Mercury)

P

Paloma dove

R

Radinka playful
Raphaela God's health, archangel

S

Sai intelligence
Sally diminutive of Sara
Sara/Sarah contentious princess

T

Tammy twin
Thalia muse of poetry/comedy
Thomasa/Thomasina twin

V

Vivienne/Vivian/Vivia lively, vivacious

100 Names for **Gemini** Boys

A

Abel breath, vapour
Alber agile mind
Alvin/Alwyn friend of the elf
Amos bearer or messenger of God
Anarawd eloquent
Ariel Shakespearean spirit of air
Arlyn swift like the cascade
Auriga charioteer

B

Baird singer, poet
Bona messenger
Brice/Bryce speckled

C

Callum/Calum dove
Carbury charioteer
Carl alternative form of Charles
Casey vigilant
Charles free man
Christopher patron saint of travellers
Clark learned, clergyman
Coleman dove
Colin dove, young chieftain

D

Dalziel I dare
Dexter skilful
Dovel young dove
Duan/Duane poem or song
Dyer colourer of fabrics

E

Earl/Earle keen intelligence
Ebert active mind
Eddy unresting
Elmo amiable
Elvan quick-willed
Elvert variable
Emil/Emile striving, industrious, rival
Emmet/Emmett industrious
Engelbert bright messenger
Enoch teacher
Erastus amiable
Erbert always alert
Erlon elfish

F

Fabron he who works with his hands
Farman traveller
Filibert flashing will
Findal inventive
Findlay capable
Francis/Frank free, from France
Franklin/Franklyn free man
Frewen free friend
Fulbert bright, shining

G

Galen healer
Galvin sparrow
Gilland bold youth
Gwyn/Gwynn white, blessed

H

Hagbert skilful
Haines self-help
Hal healthy
Hamal carrier
Harper harpist
Hasaka jester
Hastings swift
Heilyn cup-bearer
Hermes Hermes, Mercury
Hubbard intellectual
Hugh/Hew/Hugo mindful, thinker

I

Ishmael God heareth

J

Jabriel God's health
Jason healer
Javas swift
Jay bird-like, chattering
Joda playful
Jonah/Jonas dove
Jovita little dove
Jubalus lute player
Junius born in June (partly of Gemini)

K

Keenan sharp
Keith wind

L

Laris cheerful
Latimer interpreter
Levander wind
Loring instructive

M

Macaire happy
Malachi God's messenger
Michael archangel
Mick/Micky diminutives of Michael
Mike diminutive of Michael

N

Nathan/Nathaniel God has given, messenger of God
Nodin wind
Notus south wind

P

Paget little page
Patera bird
Pythias enquiring

R

Raphael God's health, archangel
Reece swift
Russell fox, cunning

S

Scott traveller from Scotland
Simon hearkening to God, he who hears

T

Tate great talker
Thomas twin, doubter
Todd fox, cunning

V

Valentine strong, healthy
Vivian lively

Z

Zivan lively

Cancer

♋ (The Crab)

21 June to **22 July**

Emotional, sensitive, always variable, Cancer people – and especially Cancer children – can laugh and cry at the same time. One moment you can have a tearful tantrum, the next a loony fit of the giggles! In their search for emotional security, Cancers come to love their home. They love their families, their community and, often, their country as well. Because these things are so precious, and because only they know how hurtful the big, cruel world can be at times, Cancers often build a protective shell around themselves. Later, this drive towards protection can extend right out to the building of financial and business empires and to becoming figures of great power. Ruled by the Moon, Cancer people often have a strong affinity with the sea – if not actually wanting to be on it, then at least gazing at its turbulent surface … reminding them of their own emotions, perhaps?

Ruling Planet

Cancer is ruled by the Moon – the Queen of the Night and the great feminine principle of nature. It is stately, noble and mysterious. Deeply sensitive and changeable, Moon people reflect the moods of their surroundings very accurately, picking up on the feelings in others and reacting quickly and intuitively to changes.

Element

Cancer is a Cardinal, Water sign, possessing great powers of emotional strength and endurance. With these credentials, Cancerians can inspire and lead whole communities – and often do. Moreover, they lead by example, and by appealing to the feelings of others.

Physical Characteristics

Cancerians often have round, moon-like faces, with dreamy, 'swimmy' eyes full of emotion. The boys can have a shell-like forehead and their movements may be slow and deliberate.

Health

Perhaps because of its emotional nature, Cancer relates closely to the stomach. Indigestion and tummy upsets of all kinds can be a problem. Psychosomatic illnesses can often develop, too, brought on by emotional strain.

Famous Cancerians

Edward, Duke of Windsor
(Abdicated English king, born 23 June 1894)

George Orwell
(Author, born 25 June 1903)

Diana, Princess of Wales
(Born 1 July 1961)

Pamela Anderson
(Actress, born 1 July 1967)

Jerry Hall
(Model, born 2 July 1960)

Tom Cruise
(Actor, born 3 July 1962)

Bill Haley
(Singer, born 6 July 1925)

Yul Brynner
(Actor, born 11 July 1915)

Lucky Connections

Gemstones	Colours	Plants	Metal
pearl	soft blue	white rose	silver
white coral	green	lily	
moonstone	sea colours	rue	

Raising a **Cancer** Child

Have you ever looked up at the Moon one night and then, a couple of nights later, looked up again? It changes. And if you have anyone in your family born under the sign of Cancer, and therefore ruled by the Moon, you will have noticed the similarity straight away. The infectious laughter or tragic tears of these little crabs as they emerge or retreat into and out of their tough shell will be a never-ending source of amazement. Because the Cancer moods go very deep indeed, they can also sometimes appear rather irritable – or 'crabby' – without any obvious reason. Perhaps it was something you said ages ago, because Cancerians have memories that go way back, and rarely forget a slight or insult. The shell includes their home, of course. They love their comforts and the security that a warm, loving home provides – and they adore their mothers, too. Later on, and no matter how many years may pass or how far away the Cancerian might travel, home cooking and a warm cuddle will always draw them back in times of crisis.

Cancer in the family home

There is nothing in life more important to Cancer than home and family. These are the home-lovers par excellence. They can play happily in their rooms for hours, deep in their own fantasy world, or they can cuddle up by the fire, watching television, blissfully content for just as long. Tender, dreamy, wanting so much to be liked, they are never happier than when everyone gets together in the home to share their feelings and wishes. They get on best with their fellow Water signs, Scorpio and Pisces, but also quite well with Virgo and Taurus.

Friendship

Always open to friendships, Cancerians treasure loyalty and kindness, and when they find a true friend they keep them for life – clinging to those they love, but discarding quickly anyone who is cruel or uncaring. Although sometimes solitary, Cancer children ultimately need the emotional stimulation of mixing with others – though this is often a tempestuous process, a tendency that certainly does not abate with the onset of teenage years. This is worth bearing in mind, because the crab can produce a nasty nip when threatened or upset!

School

Because of their retentive memories, Cancer children can handle all those history lessons full of dates of battles and kings and queens with ease. If the subject interests them, they can excel, but by the same token they can be put off easily if the teachers are unkind. If there seems to be trouble in learning any subject, or with school generally, check whether there is a problem with any of the teachers, or with bullying by other children. Despite their femininity, the girls can be every bit as physically strong and active in sports as their male counterparts, and make fine team leaders or prefects.

Hobbies and interests

Don't be disturbed if the girls want to fit into the traditional feminine role very early on – with dolls' houses, and playing at mother. Later, they might well join the boys in going farther afield and establishing their own little empire out in the community, but the great lunar, feminine principle remains ever-present. Even the boys will treasure their own private space – the 'den', garden shed or hobby room – somewhere to enjoy those quieter moments of introspection.

Choosing a Name for **Cancer**

In understanding Cancer and choosing a name, we have to recognize the overriding importance of the Moon. Here we are looking at one of the great symbols of ancient mythology and folklore which, along with the Sun, has consistently appeared as a kind of divine sister/brother pairing, a negative/positive, Yin/Yang polarity that can be found across almost all cultures, at all times. The Moon, with its monthly cycle from crescent to full, then back to old-moon crescent again, has always been venerated and prized as the great female entity of the natural world. So we have the major figures of Greek and Roman mythology Artemis and Diana, the virgin huntress, or the great female deities that preside over the sea such as Nina or Selena. Cancer and the Moon also preside over the home and relate intimately to the whole field of motherhood, families, communities, and the sense of belonging and protection that all these provide. This is why the sign of Cancer is equally important for the boys, since it often signifies those who gain popularity or notoriety in the public arena. Cancer men are often much admired and trusted by their fellows and this popularity is also a feature of any astrological chart with a strongly placed Moon. Names such as Kim, meaning 'chief', or Terry, meaning 'well-respected', are therefore suitable.

The Moon has the lily as its flower and the pearl its gemstone, so apart from the obvious Lilian and Pearl as name choices, we have the enduring Margaret, meaning 'pearl', from which numerous derivatives have developed including Maggie, Madge, Peggy, Megan and more. In fact, the Moon and its associations with night provide us with some of the most poetic and beautiful of female names, such as the lovely Lunetta, 'little moon', or Drusilla, 'watered by the dew'.

But it's not all lilies and moonshine. The flip side of the gentle, dreamy Moon goddess is the formidable mythological figure of Diana. Diana was a fierce huntress, and a staunch virgin who was wont to take very firm action against anyone violating her privacy. We therefore have numerous associations with the hunt when considering the symbolism of Cancer, including the forest and its beasts, the bear and the deer, or the accoutrements of the hunt such as the hounds or the bow and arrow (the crescent-shaped bow being an additional lunar symbol). So, in the accompanying lists you will find not only Hunter as a name for the boys but also Montgomery, meaning 'huntsman', and Hayward, 'dweller by the dark forest'. Then there is Ivor, 'bow bearer', and even Talbot, the name once given to a famous stock of bloodhounds. For the girls we have the names Diana, Cynthia or Della – all of which are derived from the classical virgin huntress of mythology and folklore.

The region of the north, and of the impenetrable forests in many European countries, has always been associated with the Water element. Names that suggest a chieftain from these regions have been included in the boys' list, including Norman, 'divine man from the north', and Norris 'north king'. Similarly, the link between the Moon, the tides and therefore shipping and trade was established fairly early on in most seafaring cultures. In astrological tradition, therefore, seamen, merchants and traders, have always been placed under the rulership of the Moon, so names such as Cramer or Mercer, both meaning 'merchant', are worthy choices, too.

100 Names for **Cancer** Girls

A

Aeron bright queen
Alcina sea maiden
Alice/Alicia noble maid
Alison alternative form of Alice
Allie diminutive of Alice
Amaris child of the moon
Angharad much-loved
Ann/Anna/Anne/Annette grace, favoured
Annabel beautiful Ann
Antoinette esteemed family
Antonia alternative form of Antoinette
Anouska/Anushka alternative forms of Ann
Artema moon goddess
Artemis huntress, lunar deity
Atalanta huntress

B

Bernadette bold bear
Bernessa of the bear
Bertha bright, famous

C

Chandra goddess brighter than stars
Coral from the sea
Coralie coral
Cordelia jewel of the sea
Cresentia of the half-moon
Cynthia alternative form of Artemis

D

Dara pearl of wisdom
Davina/Davinia beloved
Delia/Della from Delos, home of Artemis
Diana goddess of the moon, huntress
Diane/Dianne alternative forms of Diana
Donabella beautiful lady
Donna lady
Doris sea goddess
Drusilla watered by the dew

E

Emma whole, universal
Etta ruler of the home

F

Ffion alternative form of Fiona
Fiona white, fair

G

Galatea sea nymph
Gina silvery
Glenis/Glenys good, pure
Graine/Grania affectionate, love
Greta/Gretchen alternative forms of Margaret
Guinevere fair wife, white wave
Gwendolen white bow
Gwyneth blessed, happiness

H

Harriet/Hattie mistress of the home
Hendrika ruler of the home
Henrietta/Henriette ruler of the home
Hertha goddess of fertility
Hestia goddess of the hearth

I

Ilythia goddess of childbirth

J

Jarita motherly devotion
Jennifer alternative form of Guinevere
Jenny diminutive of Jennifer
June month (partly of Cancer)

L

Leyla night
Lida people's love
Lilian/Lily purity, flower (of Moon)
Lilybelle beautiful Lily
Luna goddess of the half-moon
Lunetta little moon

M

Mabel lovely, mirth
Madge/Maggie diminutives of Margaret
Madra mother
Mahsa little moon
Margaret/Margarete/Margarita pearl
Margery/Marjorie alternative forms of Margaret
Margot diminutive of Margaret
Marina sea-maiden
Marisa/Marissa star of the sea
Martha lady
Medita reflective
Meg/Megan/Meghan diminutives of Margaret
Morgan great queen, sea bright
Muriel/Meryl sea bright, fragrant

N

Naida water nymph
Neoma new moon
Nina goddess of the sea
Nydia homemaker

P

Pearl/Perlita gemstone (of the Moon)
Peggy diminutive of Margaret
Philomena/Filomena daughter of light
Phoebe shining, moon goddess

Q

Queena noble consort, queen

R

Reanna moon goddess or nymph
Regan/Regina queen
Rita diminutive of Margaret
Rose white rose (of the Moon)
Rosina sea rose

S

Selena/Selina moonlight, moon goddess
Shohan pearl
Sian alternative form of June
Silver metal (of the Moon)
Silvia/Sylvia of the forest
Sonia wise one
Sue/Susan/Susannah white lily
Suzette little lily

T

Toni diminutive of Antonia

U

Ula jewel of the sea
Ursula she-bear

V

Vesta goddess of the family hearth

W

Wendy diminutive of Gwendolen

100 Names for **Cancer** Boys

A

Aahmes child of the moon
Alworth respected by all
Anthony/Antony esteemed family, highly praised
Arlin sea bound
Arthur bear man, noble
Atherton dweller in the forest

B

Bainbridge of the sea
Berman keeper of bears
Bernard bold bear
Bevis bow

C

Cavanagh handsome
Chapman merchant
Conroy hound of the plain
Cramer merchant

D

Darrell/Daryl darling
David beloved
Derby place of the deer
Derek/Derik/Derrick people's ruler
Dirk alternative form of Derek
Dmitri from Demeter, goddess of the harvest

E

Eamon alternative form of Edward
Edward guardian of property, fortunate
Elton Ella's settlement
Ervand sea warrior

F

Foster forester

G

Gilman big man
Graham great homestead, grey manor
Griswold from the wild forest

H

Hamlyn home-lover
Hamo/Haymo home
Harding brave, strong, hardy
Hardy alternative form of Harding
Harley deer hunter
Hartley dweller by the lea of the stags
Hayward guardian/dweller by the ledge or dark forest
Henry ruler of the home
Hogan eminent
Hume home-lover
Hunter huntsman

I

Ivor bow bearer

K

Kelwin dweller by the water
Kenaz hunter
Kim chief

L

Lambert his country's glory
Lingard sea guard

Emotional Intuitive **Protective**

M

Magna the coming moon
Matthew gift of God
Melva chief
Mercer merchant
Meredith sea protector
Merlin hill by the sea
Merton from near the sea
Mervin/Mervyn raven of the sea
Montgomery huntsman
Morgan sea bright
Morven seaman
Moses drawn from the water
Murdoch/Murdock seaman
Murphy sea warrior
Murray seaman

N

Nestor he who remembers
Norman man from the north
Norris north king
Norvin man of the north
Norwood north wood

O

Orlando alternative form of Roland
Osborne sacred bear
Oscar friend of deer, godly spear
Owen well-born

R

Raymond good protector
Reginald well-counselled ruler
Reynaud/Reynold alternative forms of Reginald
Roderick rich in fame
Roger/Rodger praise
Roland/Rowland fame of the land
Roscoe sea horse
Royce chief
Royston settlement of Royce

S

Samuel heard of God
Seaforth peaceful conqueror
Seaton dweller by the sea
Sebastian venerable
Selmar rolling sea
Seth appointed
Seward warden of the sea coast
Sherwood sea ruler
Silas of the forest
Silva of the forest
Silvester/Sylvester forest dweller
Sofian devoted

T

Talbot stock of bloodhounds
Tedman patriot
Terry well-respected
Thaddeus wise praise
Theodore divine gift
Timothy divine honour, respect
Tony diminutive of Anthony

W

Walden/Waldo mighty
Winston dweller in a friendly town
Woodrow houses by the wood, popular
Woody alternative form of Woodrow

Leo

♌ (The Lion)

23 July to **22 August**

Leos are the extroverts of life. They are not only very good-looking, but also highly exciting and interesting people. Yes, of course they are – you just ask them! Even if they don't quite carry off the charismatic leader role, they will at least like to think that they could, some day, if they needed to. Leos thrive on being noticed and thought of in glowing terms: reputation is all. And as long as it is at their bidding, at just the time and place that suits them (usually when they have donned their most fashionable clothes or have all their make-up on), they just adore being the centre of attention. Smart cars, jewellery, fine furnishings, display of all kinds are important, because Leos – and this is the key – are proud, dignified creatures who like to surround themselves with beauty. Above all, they love style.

Ruling Planet

Leos are ruled by the creative force of the resplendent Sun. Basking in the sunshine of life, they exude their own special kind of warmth and vitality. The Sun is fertile, energizing and brilliant – and every Leo, no matter how untypically humble, aspires to these qualities.

Element

Leo is a powerful Fire sign – the source of those famous inspirational, creative abilities that can transform the lion's surroundings with such panache. The additional Fixed nature of the sign, however, also bestows a certain obstinacy.

Physical Characteristics

Leos have an upright stance, with a long, flexible spine – like a big cat. The 'mane' is usually obvious, too, with lots of pride taken in their hair, which is often rich and curly or swept back. Similarly, the boys often have 'whiskers' in which they take great pride.

Health

Leos are robust, but may be prone to sudden, feverish complaints. They are excitable and their hearts can race. This sign rules the heart, and if the fire and romance ever go out of their life, Leos can become lethargic, even lazy, leading to obesity.

Famous Leos

George Bernard Shaw
(Playwright, born 26th July 1856)

Mick Jagger
(Singer, songwriter, born 26th July 1943)

Jacqueline Onassis
(Wife of J.F. Kennedy, born 28th July 1929)

Alfred Hitchcock
(Film director, born 13th August 1899)

Napoleon Bonaparte
(French Emperor, born 15th August 1769)

Madonna
(Singer and actress, born 16th August 1958)

Mae West
(Actress, born 17th August 1892)

Robert Redford
(Actor, born 18th August 1937)

Lucky Connections

Gemstones	Colours	Plants	Metal
amber	orange	sunflower	gold
topaz	yellow	laurel	
ruby	gold	marigold	
		St John's wort	
		peony	

Raising a **Leo** Child

The typical Leo child will have a sunny, friendly disposition. Proud and sometimes rather vain, Leos of any age usually enjoy being the centre of attention, and can therefore easily fall into the role of 'king pin' or 'queen bee', having favourites and devoted admirers – or else allowing themselves to be waited upon by others and becoming rather lazy as a consequence. Being seriously into designer labels, they do like to be thought of as rather special and, if allowed to, will squander their pocket money on luxury items and display. Romance is also a big thing in any Leo's life, and even at an early age their emotions can be turbulent as relationships come and go, often with alarming rapidity. The girls can go through a tomboy phase, while the boys may sometimes have moments of untypical introversion and shyness when nursing a 'wounded paw'. There is nothing sadder than the sight of a Leo whose pride has been dented. Conversely, there is nothing more joyful or inspirational than a Leo on top form. These are the trendsetters of the zodiac, the creative, ideas people, full of fun and games.

Leo in the family home

Leos are most comfortable when in charge of the situation, so they're just great in an emergency, should one arise – and one usually does when Leos are let loose. You will find yourself busy with lots of entertaining when Leos are holding court. At such times, they will insist on polite and courteous behaviour from their guests, as well as loyalty and honesty, and will not suffer fools easily. They usually get on best with their fellow Fire signs, Aries and Sagittarius, but also quite well with the Air signs, Gemini and Libra.

Friendship

With their good looks (don't ever tell them they aren't good-looking) and cheerful personalities, Leos naturally draw people to them. They like their playmates to be outgoing but also suitably deferential, tending to drop anyone who fails to show due appreciation. They can also become quite sulky and morose if made fun of or if they feel someone is being disloyal. Also, don't forget, you may have one of those notoriously quiet 'pussycats', the brave lions that really would love to be the life and soul of the party but are simply too shy.

School

Leos enjoy the limelight at school and respond well to a challenge and to a balance of affection, respect and discipline, with plenty of praise for their accomplishments. The influence these proud and fearless personalities can exert over others makes them extremely successful in positions of authority. Their ability to see the whole picture quickly and intuitively, and to delegate responsibility, makes them excellent team leaders and school prefects. However, because they can easily influence others, they can also sometimes lead their group or team into difficulties. They shine at subjects such as art, in which their work is seen or displayed in one way or another.

Hobbies and interests

Leos enjoy many kinds of physical activity, including sports and games. If there is some degree of style attached to these, so much the better! Activities such as tennis, dancing, driving, running, motor racing, drama, parties and eating out will all be high on the agenda. Leos can also be creative beings. Music, colour and romance – these are the things that are closest to a Leo's heart, no matter how young or old.

Choosing a Name for **Leo**

Leos are very special people, remember? You will need to keep this firmly in mind when choosing a name. Names that reflect the warmth, glory and splendour of the Sun are obvious choices, and because of Leo's pretensions to the regal life, any of the traditional names of kings or queens are also eminently suitable.

Throughout history, successful warriors, noble families or clans would choose names that meant 'brave leader' or 'great man', or which suggested having somehow received the favour of the gods. These people wanted to give the impression of status and worth. They were the 'anointed ones', the chosen mediators between the supernatural and mundane worlds. Take, for instance, the name Aaron, meaning no less than 'descended from the gods'! More modestly, perhaps, there was the wish simply to give praise to the gods. For example, the name of the supreme god of the old testament, Jehovah, has percolated down to us in names such as Joshua and Joseph. The simple form of Joe has also come via this root, as has one of the most enduring and popular of all names, John.

The Sun, ruler of Leo, with its obvious abundance of life-force, was invariably associated with kingship, but also with the chief among any grouping of creatures. The lion is king of all the beasts, so our lists contain a legion of Leo derivatives including Lionel, Leon and Leonard, along with feminine versions such as Leonora, Leona and Leonie. Other names that relate to the chief of a species in nature are also suitable: the rose, being the most regal of flowers, is employed extensively in heraldry and is grown around castles, palaces and on royal estates throughout the world. Rose, therefore, is an excellent choice of name for a Leo girl, along with her many derivatives which include the lovely Rosamund, Rosabel and Roseanne.

In the fascinating world of Greek mythology, the Sun is associated either with the special divinity of Helios – from which we derive names such as Helen – or else the great Olympian god Apollo. Apollo epitomises not only the qualities of masculine strength and physical proportion but also governs the arts, such as music and poetry. He was very fond of the nymph Daphne (see girls names). Daphne, however, being perhaps not so smitten, and while being chased one day by her distinguished admirer, chose to have herself transformed into a laurel tree. Thereafter, Apollo chose to wear a crown of laurels in her memory. Heroes of war or victors in the games were also crowned with laurels in honour of Apollo. It is from this source that we derive names such as Laura, for the girls, or Lawrence, for the boys, both meaning 'victorious, crowned with laurels'.

Finally, names that reflect the colours or gemstones favoured by Leo would also be a natural choice – so there is Topaz, Amber or Ruby for the girls and the more unusual Orwin or Goldwyn, meaning 'golden friend' or 'gold friend', or Boyd, meaning 'yellow-haired', for the boys. Above all, you need to give your little Leo a name to be proud of, and one that is not too obscure, nor too common either. Kingly or queenly names are the exception to this rule, however: they are often quite ordinary, yet always possess that air of authority and class which sets them apart. An excellent example of this is the ever-popular John (or its feminine derivatives Joan, Joanne and Joanna), meaning 'God has favoured' or 'grace of God'. This should be enough to satisfy the most lofty of Leo aspirations. After all, you can't go much higher than that!

100 Names for **Leo** Girls

A

Aamor sunbeam
Ada noble
Aileen alternative form of Helen
Albertina bright, illustrious
Almira princess
Amber jewel, resin (of the Sun)
Apollonia from Apollo, Sun
Ariel lion of God
Augustine great, venerable, of August
Aurea/Aurelia/Aureola golden one

C

Caltha marigold
Calvina bright-haired
Canda brightness
Candice/Candace glowing
Cleodora glorious gift
Cleopatra from a famous father
Clorinda renowned
Cordelia from the heart
Crispina curly-headed

D

Danielle God has judged, of lions
Daphne laurel, beloved of Apollo (Sun)
Delphia/Delphine of the oracle at Delphi
Denise from Dionysus, god of wine
Devina divine

E

Earlene noble woman
Eileen bright, radiant
Elaine alternative form of Helen
Eleanor alternative form of Helen
Electra amber, radiant
Eliana/Eliane from the sun

Ella/Ellie diminutives of Helen
Ellen/Ellenis alternative forms of Helen
Erma noble maid
Erminia regal
Ethel noble
Eugenie noble born

F

Fresa curly-haired

G

Gilda gilded
Gloria glory
Goldie of gold

H

Hafwen fair summer
Hanna/Hannah grace, favoured
Helen/Helena shining one
Helianthe sunflower
Heloise alternative form of Helen
Heulwen sunshine

J

Jane/Jayne God has favoured, grace of God
Janet little Jane, little one of divine grace
Jean/Jeanette alternative forms of Jane
Joan alternative form of Jane
Joanna/Joanne alternative forms of Jane

L

Laura victorious, crowned with laurels
Laureen/Lauryn alternative forms of Laura
Lauren/Loren alternative forms of Laura
Laurette alternative form of Laura
Laurissa alternative form of Laura
Lea/Leah gazelle-like
Lena alternative form of Helen
Lenice brave as a lion
Lenka light
Leona brave as lion
Leonie lion
Leonora alternative form of Eleanor
Lucia/Lucy light
Lucille alternative form of Lucinda
Lucinda bright, shining

M

Marigold flower (of Leo)
Meingolda my golden flower
Michaela likened to God
Michelle alternative form of Michaela
Mora/Morag the sun

N

Nell/Nellie/Nelly diminutives of Helen

O

Oriel golden

Q

Queena noble consort, queen

R

Regan queen, regal
Reine queen
Rhoda/Rhode alternative forms of Rose
Roberta bright, famous
Robina alternative form of Roberta
Rosabel beautiful rose
Rosalie/Rosetta little rose
Rosalind/Rosalinda alternative forms of Rose
Rosamund alternative form of Rose
Rosanne/Roseanne rose of grace
Rose regal flower
Roselle little rose
Rosemarie/Rosemary herb/flower (of the Sun)
Rozene alternative form of Rose
Ruby gemstone (of Leo)

S

Sarah princess
Sheena/Shayna alternative forms of Jane
Shirley bright clearing
Sian alternative form of Jane
Siobhan alternative form of Jane
Stef/Steph/Stevie diminutives of Stephanie
Stephanie garland, crown
Sula Sun
Sulwyn fair as the Sun

T

Tabitha graceful gazelle
Topaz gemstone (of Leo)

U

Ulrica/Ulrika noble ruler

Z

Zara/Zarah brightness, splendour

100 Names for **Leo** Boys

A

Aaron descended from the gods, mountain
Aidan Celtic Sun god, fire
Albert/Adelbert nobly bright
Anders/Andreas courageous
Antol estimable
Arthur noble
Augustine great
Augustus great, venerable, of August
Austin/Austen alternative forms of Augustine

B

Basil royal
Berthold ruling in splendour
Boyd yellow-haired
Brett upright

C

Cebert bright
Cleon glorious
Clydias glorious
Crispin/Crispian curly headed

D

Daniel God has judged, of lions
Dempsey proud
Denis/Dennis from Dionysus, god of wine
Dwight alternative form of Denis

E

Egbert eminently bright
Elmer noble, famous
Elroy regal
Emerson powerful, rich
Emery alternative form of Emerson
Eric kingly, powerful
Eugene well born, noble

F

Fulbert shining bright

G

Garland crown, wreath
Gene diminutive of Eugene
Gilbert bright pledge
Goldwin/Goldwyn gold friend

H

Haima made of gold
Hakan fiery
Herbert man of brilliance
Howell eminent
Hubert bright

I

Iain/Ian alternative forms of John
Ivan alternative form of John

J

Jermyn bright
Jesse wealthy
Jethro abundance
Jock alternative form of John
Joel Jehovah is God
John/Johnny God has favoured, grace of God
Jonathan/Jonny alternative forms of John
Joseph may the Lord add
Joshua the Lord is salvation

K

Kai king
Kalo/Kalon royal
Kemble royally bold
King king, chief
Kingley king's meadow

Bright Energetic **Bold**

L

Lars lord
Laurence/Lawrence laurel
Lennox/Lenox chieftain
Leo lion
Leon nature of the lion
Leonard brave as a lion
Leonidas lion-like
Leopold bold for the people
Leroy king
Lionel little lion
Lorus alternative form of Laurence
Lucian/Lucien alternative forms of Luke
Lucius bringer of light
Luke light

M

Magnus great, regal
Matthew gift of Jehovah
Max diminutive of Maximilian
Maximilian greatest
Melchior king of light

N

Nolan noble

O

Orwin golden friend
Osbert brightness of God

P

Philibert brilliant

R

Rab bright fortune
Rex king
Reyner kingly
Robert bright, famous
Robin alternative form of Robert
Roddy/Rod alternative forms of Roderick
Roderic/Roderick rich in fame
Roy king

S

Sampson/Samson/Sanson splendid Sun
Savero bright
Sean/Shane/Shaun/Shawn alternative forms of John
Sol sun
Steafan/Stefan/Steffan alternative forms of Stephan
Stephan/Stephen/Steven garland, crown
Sulwyn Sun fair

T

Theodore gift from God
Tiernan kingly
Timon honourable
Tobias the Lord is good
Torbert bright eminence

Z

Zac/Zach/Zack/Zak diminutives of Zacharias
Zacharias/Zachary remembered of Jehovah
Zerah rising light

Virgo

♍ (The Virgin)

23 August to **22 September**

The thing about Virgos of any age is that they know what's best – they really do. You may think that lovely pair of socks is just perfect, but your little Virgo will disagree; you may think the meal you have just prepared is highly nutritious, but your little Virgo will demur. They are fussy, it's true, but in time this trait will blossom into qualities of discernment, moderation and realism. Neat, meticulous and blessed with more than their fair share of common sense, Virgos have an astonishing ability to focus on detail and see projects through to the end. Above all, you can rely on them. They may not seek the spotlight socially or be the life and soul of the party, but they are genuine and kind, usually loyal, and conscientious in their chosen career. Health issues interest them, as does anything relating to crafts or collecting.

Ruling Planet

Virgo is ruled by Mercury, the winged messenger of the gods. Mercury alone is usually volatile and busy, but in association with Virgo becomes more stable. This is a temperate combination, tending towards industry, thrift and dependability.

Element

Virgo belongs to the Earth element and is also a Mutable sign. Steady, thoughtful, and above all sensible, Earth signs are celebrated for their quiet, unassuming strength and integrity – and Virgo is no exception. Their feet are planted firmly on the ground.

Physical Characteristics

Neat, tidy and precise in their ways, Virgos are often reserved in nature, with head slightly bowed. There is a certain debonair, classical look about them, though just occasionally an awkward gait.

Health

The meticulous Virgo personality can sometimes overdo cleanliness to the point of becoming even more susceptible to the viral and bacterial infections they so studiously seek to avoid. The bowels are often delicate.

Famous Virgos

Sean Connery
(Actor, born 25 August 1930)

Mother Teresa of Calcutta
(born 27 August 1910)

Sir Richard Attenborough
(Film director, born 29 August 1923)

Peter Sellers
(Actor, born 8 September 1925)

Hugh Grant
(Actor, born 9 September 1960)

Lauren Bacall
(Actress, born 16 September 1924)

Samuel Johnson
(Compiler of first dictionary, born 18 September 1709)

Jeremy Irons
(Actor, born 19 September 1948)

Lucky Connections

Gemstones	Colours	Plants	Metal
agate	grey	iris	mercury
beryl	brown	elderflower	(quicksilver)
onyx	white	hazel	
	mixtures	myrtle	

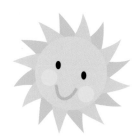

Raising a **Virgo** Child

Uncannily well-behaved, Virgo children are usually easy to manage compared to their more egotistic cousins of the zodiac. They have their own agenda when it comes to most things, and their own particular tastes and preferences. And because they really do like to 'get it right' and not make fools of themselves, they will listen and learn whenever given a logical explanation for how things should be done. Tidiness is second nature to most Virgos – even children – so you will not only find their rooms in order but might also be told off yourself if you change things around without asking permission. Everything has its proper place, and will be filed away and catalogued by that famously neat Virgo brain. They feel secure with order and routine, and are frightened of doing things out of turn – or of anything that might draw attention to themselves or embarrass them. They need to have the right change for the bus, clean shoes – and please do make sure the ironing is ready on time, with no creases!

Virgo in the family home

Virgo children appreciate privacy and space, somewhere to listen to their own thoughts – perhaps a quiet room or study, or anywhere they can arrange their busy little heads and make sense of life. This is important. Remember, they don't like things out of place – including information – or any nasty shocks or surprises. Moreover, they really can be incredibly adult about things, and will appreciate the chance to talk over any difficulties quietly on a one-to-one basis. Among the family, they enjoy best the company of their fellow Earth signs, Taurus and Capricorn, but also get on quite well with Cancer and Scorpio.

Friendship

Virgo children are certainly not show-offs in any sense. Modest and unassuming, they value the company of a few close friends rather than large crowds, so parties or school discos might not feature too highly on their list of priorities. They are not in the least impressed by nonsense of any kind, and prefer people to behave sensibly when they are in their company. A lot of other children appreciate this behaviour, too, and so come to value the good counsel of Virgos in times of crisis.

School

The demanding world of school and academia is generally no threat to little Virgos. Unless they are manifestly unhappy at school because of bullying or disruptive classmates, they will work quietly and efficiently towards their goal, be it exams or homework. And if they are ever accused of becoming teacher's pet, it is just because they find it easy to communicate with adults, and vice versa. If they are persuaded to take part in sports, they are best in a team rather than assuming the mantle of leadership.

Hobbies and interests

The word 'hobby' was probably invented for Virgos. They are life's born collectors and can happily lose themselves for hours, if not days, engrossed in their current hobby or interest. This could be stamps, toys, or football memorabilia – almost anything – and they will go to enormous lengths to acquire that last piece! Computers are ideal companions for these busy little people, and the special mercurial intellect of Virgo is usually brilliant not only at working with them, but probably at programming and repairing them as well. These little Virgo geniuses are very handy, and every home should have one!

Choosing a Name for **Virgo**

In selecting a name for a Virgo child, especially a girl, we are utterly spoilt for choice, and in the list given here you will find some of the great feminine names such as Mary, Elizabeth and Katherine. These are not simply feminine versions of masculine names, by the way – such as Charlene coming from Charles, or Joan from John – but unique female names in their own right. It is perhaps no accident, therefore, that some of their owners have become the great historical icons of feminine power and authority: Catherine the Great of Russia, the Virgin Mary and Queen Elizabeth I, the great 'Virgin Queen' of England.

In fact, Elizabeth is typical of many ancient names in its meaning, 'oath of God' or 'God has sworn'. What do these rather obscure phrases signify for us today? Perhaps they are telling us that when we receive the wonderful gift of a new life we still have our side of the bargain to keep, in serving God by raising the child responsibly, with kindness and love.

For some, the sign of the Virgin might seem a rather dull one to be born under these days. Not a bit of it! Virgo embraces the powerful pagan influences of the mighty earth goddess – including, perhaps most important of all, Demeter. Demeter is the Greek goddess of the harvest, and her story in mythology, so deeply entwined with that of her daughter Kore, draws us towards some of the most profound and mystical of ideas. A tale that has survived the centuries, represented in art and literature the world over, it tells us that life and renewal can only come from some measure of self-sacrifice. This is why in many of the earlier drawings or woodcuts depicting Virgo you will find a woman holding an ear of corn in her hand – this is the harvest, the ending of one life-cycle in order that another might begin from its seed.

All of this rather seems to put the poor Virgo boys somewhat in the shade. Nevertheless, there are still some excellent choices, not necessarily drawing on the virtues of chastity but looking instead to the industry and intelligence often typified by this sign. For instance, many sources associate Virgo with the Greek god Hephaestus, the lame blacksmith and craftsman to the gods, or with the powerful Nordic Thor. These are not themselves names that many of us would choose, but there is Claude – always popular even though it means 'lame' – and Dustin, meaning 'Thor's stone'. This stone probably signifies either the anvil or a thunderbolt, both references to the potent idea of fire tamed for the service of humankind. In the Christian tradition meanwhile, there is Christopher, the 'bearer of Christ' as he forded the stream, which again hints at service and patience.

The idea of 'service' being a worthy activity sometimes seems odd to modern ears, sounding rather menial. However, the term is still used quite commonly when, for example, powerful people such as politicians state that they 'serve the people' (and thereby lead). Virgo has always been associated with the ideas of true modesty and service, and therefore we find names referring to practitioners of medicine, such as Jason or Asa, both meaning 'healer' and others relating to the crafts or professions, like Swain, 'youth in service' or Wayne, 'cartwright'.

By the same token, the traditional biblical names of the servants of the word of God, such as Luke or Matthew, are eminently suitable, the former being also the name of the patron saint of doctors. Even in his more sombre manifestation, Mercury bestows an interest in the healing arts, and Virgo is often to be found here, working away quietly with dedication and modesty for the good of others.

100 Names for **Virgo** Girls

A

Adara virgin
Agatha good
Agnes chaste, pure
Aida modesty
Althea to heal
Amelia industrious

B

Beata blessed
Beatrice/Beatrix blessed, joyful
Benedicta/Benice blessed
Bess/Bet/Betty diminutives of Elizabeth
Bridget/Brigitte strength, virtue

C

Cathy diminutive of Katherine
Catriona alternative form of Katherine
Chastina pure, chaste
Claudia lame (as Hephaestus)
Cora/Corinna maiden
Coyne reserved, modest

D

Damasa damsel, maid
Danella wise mistress
Danette wise little mistress
Demeter goddess of the harvest
Docila/Docilla willing to learn
Donella little maid
Donna lady
Dorina perfection
Dusty from Dustin, Thor's stone

E

Elise/Ellie alternative forms of Elizabeth
Elizabeth oath of God, God has sworn
Elsa/Elsie alternative forms of Elizabeth
Elspeth alternative form of Elizabeth
Elysia of paradise, blissful
Enid purity
Erda earth goddess
Evodie she who takes the right path

F

Fabrianne maid of good works

G

Gaia earth goddess

H

Hazel plant (of Mercury)
Hebe eternal youth
Hermione maid of high degree
Honesta honourable
Honor/Honora integrity, honour

I

Irene messenger of peace
Isabel/Isabella/Isobel alternative forms of Elizabeth

K

Kalya healthy
Kalyana one who is virtuous
Karen/Karyn/Karin alternative forms of Katherine
Karena/Karina alternative forms of Katherine
Kate/Katie diminutives of Katherine
Katherine/Catherine self-sacrifice, pure
Kathleen/Katrine alternative forms of Katherine
Katinka alternative form of Katherine
Kitty diminutive of Katherine
Kore maiden, daughter of Demeter
Kyla comely

L

Lana my child
Libby alternative form of Elizabeth
Liese/Lisbeth/Lisette alternative forms of Elizabeth
Lilian pure, flower (of Mercury)
Lily diminutive of Lilian
Linda pretty, neat
Lynette/Lynn alternative forms of Linda

M

Maida maiden
Malca industrious
Maria/Marie alternative forms of Mary
Marian/Marianne alternative forms of Mary
Marilyn/Marylyn of Mary's line
Mary wished-for child, sacred virgin
Maureen alternative form of Mary
Melina gentle
Melissa bee, symbol of industry
Mena mercy
Mercedes merciful
Mercy compassion, mercy
Mia (from Maria) mine
Millicent/Millie industrious

N

Naomi pleasant one
Neysa chaste, pure
Nora/Norah honourable
Norine/Noreen honourable

O

Ola virgin, eternal, daughter

P

Paige/Page young servant, child
Parthenia virgin, maid
Pavita purified
Penelope thread, weaver
Pia pious
Polly diminutive of Mary
Prudence prudent, careful

R

Raphaela God's health
Rhea earth goddess
Rina pure

S

Sai intelligence
Samantha asked of God
Sue diminutive of Susan
Susan/Susanna/Susannah lily, pure

T

Teresa/Terese/Theresa carrier of corn, reaper
Terri/Terry diminutives of Teresa
Tess/Tessa/Tesse/Tessie alternative forms of Teresa
Tracey/Tracy alternative forms of Teresa
Trinette little maid
Trixie diminutive of Beatrice

U

Una the one, perfection

V

Verda fresh, virginal
Virginia maid, virgin

100 Names for **Virgo** Boys

A

Abdiel God's servant
Aldo servant
Ali servant
Asa doctor, healer

B

Barnabus son of consolation
Barnaby alternative form of Barnabus
Barney diminutive of Barnabus
Baxter baker
Ben diminutive of Benedict or Benjamin
Benedict blessed
Benjamin son of the right hand
Bruno brown

C

Chris diminutive of Christopher
Christopher bearer of Christ
Clark learned man, clergyman
Claude lame (as Hephaestus)
Clement merciful
Cliff/Clifford river ford
Curtis courteous
Cyril lord, saintly name

D

Dalton dweller in the vale
Dean dweller in the valley, dean
Demetrius from Demeter, goddess of the harvest
Denman man of the valley
Dermot/Dermott without envy
Diarmud/Diarmait alternative forms of Dermot
Durand/Durant enduring, lasting
Dustin Thor's stone

E

Earl/Earle of keen intelligence
Earnest/Ernest serious, earnest
Ebert of active mind
Elliot/Elliott the Lord is my God
Ellis oath of God
Elvis all-wise
Emil/Emile industrious, striving
Enoch dedicated, trained
Erhard resolution, intelligent
Ernie diminutive of Earnest
Eustace fruitful harvest, steadfast

F

Fidel faithful
Fletcher maker of arrows

G

Gabriel archangel, my strength is God
Galen healer
Gildas servant of God, gilded
Godfrey God's peace
Gordon spacious fort
Graham great (or gravelly) homestead
Guy modern usage, possibly 'guide'

H

Hadden of the moors
Hubbard alternative form of Hugh
Hugh/Hew/Hugo mindful, thinker

I

Ismael God heareth

J

Jason healer
Josiah praised, faith

Practical Focused **Supportive**

K

Kit diminutive of Christopher

L

Lance diminutive of Lancelot
Lancelot he who serves
Lane passageway
Lawton man of refinement
Lindsay/Lindsey of gentle speech
Lingard gentle guard
Luca/Lukas alternative forms of Luke
Luke apostle
Lyndon dweller on the hill by the linden tree

M

Macy bearer of the mace or sceptre
Maitland dweller in the meadow
Malachi God's messenger
Mason worker in stone
Matthew gift of God, evangelist
Medwin strong, worthy friend
Michael messenger, archangel
Mick/Mike diminutives of Michael
Millard miller
Milton mill keeper
Morton from the moor village

N

Netis trusted friend

P

Paul small, humble, modest
Pawley alternative form of Paul

R

Raphael archangel, God has healed

S

Selwyn blessed friend
Seth appointed
Shanahn sagacious, wise
Sheean courteous
Sherman wool shearer
Simon hearkening to God, he who hears
Simeon alternative form of Simon
Sinclair saintly, illustrious
Sterling little star
Stewart/Stuart steward
Swain youth in service

T

Taylor tailor
Terence tender
Thane servant
Theophilus loved of God
Titus safe, honoured
Trevor discreet, great homestead

V

Vaughan small, modest

W

Wayne cartwright, wagon
Webster he who weaves
Wesley/Westley of the west meadow
Wyatt guide

Z

Zelig blessed

Libra

♎ (The Scales)

23 September to 23 October

Libra is the sign of balance – hence the scales of justice as its emblem. For Libra, 'balance' means beauty, proportion, harmony: the cultivation of everything that brings happiness in life. Far from being self-indulgent, however, Libra usually has a passionate desire to spread this message far and wide, and seeks to solve disputes and bring concord in all places, from the family home to the community – and even the planet itself! Librans are nothing if not idealistic. These are Venus-ruled beings – charming, voluptuous, sensual. Their main difficulty lies in making decisions. When faced with choice, Librans often go into a complete tailspin. Don't rush them though! They are just figuring out the best way to go, the right path to take. Debating the pros and cons of any issue is irresistible to Librans of any age, making them lively and stimulating companions.

Ruling Planet

Libra, like Taurus, is ruled by the planet Venus. Sensuous and delightful, Venus with Libra denotes a love of beauty, harmony and proportion, but also brings with it considerable creative energy. There is an abiding love of colour and fragrance.

Element

Libra is a Cardinal, Air sign, making it extremely outward-looking and progressive. Able to communicate their needs easily, they strive towards contentment and harmony in all things. This combination also gives them the ability to lead and inspire others.

Physical Characteristics

Usually well-proportioned and comely, Librans generally cultivate an appearance of tidiness and good looks. The women are fashion conscious and elegant, and the men, too, often have a colourful dress sense, being 'dapper', with perhaps a dimple on the chin.

Health

As long as their environment is clean and peaceful, Librans enjoy good health most of the time. However, the urinary tract, kidneys, and reproductive organs can be areas of susceptibility.

Famous Librans

Michael Douglas
(Actor, born 25 September 1944)

Olivia Newton-John
(Singer and actress, born 26 September 1948)

Peter Finch
(Actor, born 28 September 1916)

Richard Harris
(Actor, born 1 October 1932)

Bob Geldof
(Singer, born 5 October 1951)

Desmond Tutu
(South African archbishop, born 7 October 1931)

John Lennon
(Singer and composer, born 9 October 1940)

Rita Hayworth
(Actress, born 17 October 1918)

Lucky Connections

Gemstones	Colours	Plants	Metal
sapphire	blue	columbine	copper
beryl	pink	violet	
lapis lazuli	pastels	plum	
		sorrel	

Raising a **Libra** Child

Your Libra child will value an environment that is peaceful, loving and soothing to its delicate little soul. Loud noises, gaudy colours or any sort of anger or violence can wound Librans deeply, so you really will need to be on your very best behaviour. On the other hand, if you do expose them to the influence of the finer things, you will find they take these up with a passion. Reality has to intervene sometimes, of course, and there is always work to be done and those difficult decisions to be made – but in the meantime, Libra children find comfort in all the good things in life, luxuriating and revelling amid flowers and perfumes, bubble baths, candles and aromatherapy oils, music and books, art and good cuisine. Just make sure that painting is not hanging crookedly on the wall, nor the television too loud! Provide your little Libra with a peaceful room, fluffy blankets and cuddly toys, and you won't go far wrong.

Libra in the family home

For Librans, home is a place of refuge from all the brashness and ugliness of the world. They are not 'sissies', but they do like to make the domestic environment somewhere special, a place of safety, warmth and comfort. Harmony surrounds them, and even young Librans will enjoy a rainy afternoon in their bedroom reading a good story or listening to their favourite music. They love this space to be personal to them, to be tidy and clean, and not invaded by their less refined siblings too often. In this, they tend to get on best with their fellow Air signs, Gemini and Aquarius, but also quite well with two of the Fire signs, Leo and Sagittarius.

Friendship

Friends for a Libra child have to be gentle and sensitive individuals. Librans do not feel at all comfortable around noisy, aggressive people and are not in the least bit impressed by threats or coercion. They need time to decide on who they want their friends to be, too – people they can trust, usually. Then, once their friendships are established, they expect fairness, equality and mutual respect to prevail – as it does in any good partnership, of course.

School

Libra children excel at artistic subjects such as literature, music, or anything involving a sense of rhythm, proportion or harmony. Mathematics often draws them for much the same reasons, and their fondness for discussion and debate makes for an abiding interest in constitutional and political subjects, too. They may need a little coaxing towards the rough-and-tumble of sports, especially if these involve getting muddy and dirty. But once this barrier has been broken (and it probably is good for them to break it occasionally), they can make formidable team players and charismatic captains, too, with excellent powers of anticipation.

Hobbies and interests

Creative subjects and artistic hobbies are food and drink to Librans. If given the opportunity, they will take up musical instruments and learn them well, become avid readers and collectors of beautiful things, and with paintbrush and colours will transform everything around them with impeccable good taste, including their bedroom walls. Smart, fashionable clothes, perfume and new hairstyles occupy their waking life, and sweet dreams and peaceful slumbers their night-time journeys.

Choosing a Name
for **Libra**

In naming your Libra child, look for those names signifying good looks or comeliness. After all, you may well have one of the up-and-coming beauties or dapper gents of the zodiac here, and there is an enormous choice in this respect: Ann, meaning 'favoured', Annabel, 'beautiful Ann', and Cherie or Cherry, 'sweet darling', for the girls; or Kenneth, meaning 'handsome', Darren, 'darling', and Finnegan, 'fair, handsome', for the boys.

However, if your taste is for something a little more exotic, why not explore the astrological connections? The morning (or evening) star, Venus, which is the ruling planet of Libra, has given rise to many delightful female names such as Esther or Estelle, derived from the earlier Ishtar, the Assyrian goddess of beauty and love. In fact, most languages have a female name for the planet Venus – our list includes the Welsh Gwendydd and the Slovakian Danica.

Bearing in mind the peace-loving nature of this sign, we can also draw upon those universal emblems of peace like the olive branch – giving us Olivia for the girls and Oliver for the boys – and the dove of peace itself, from which are derived Colman for the boys and Jemima for the girls. Female names originating in the flowers or herbs unique to Venus, which include Columbine and Violet, are likewise suitable, as indeed is any reference to floral beauty – such as Florian, meaning 'flowery', this being a name that can also be used for the boys, with the spelling altered slightly to Florean.

Venus is very much a pagan entity, and Christianity has always found it difficult to accommodate such an archetype of sensuous beauty within its own special message. But the figure of Mary Magdalene in the New Testament has eventually assumed this role, and so names such as Madeleine, Magdalen or Magdalene itself appear in our list of choices for Libra girls, along with all those names that refer indirectly to Venus and her mythological story, including the Greek Nerine, meaning 'sea born'.

On a more astrological note, the first degree of Libra, being opposite in the zodiac to Aries, marks the westernmost part of the sky, and is therefore the place of the autumnal equinox and sunset. This is reflected in names such as Autumn and the more unusual Dysis, from a Greek word meaning 'sunset'.

Words that suggest places of peace or harmony, like a meadow or clearing in the woods, give rise to several very Libra-like names, particularly for the boys. The list therefore includes names such as Lee, meaning 'peaceful meadow'. Meanwhile, concern for the welfare of their fellows and a passion for justice and equality are features of the Libra personality that often draws them towards the legal profession, so names suggesting advocacy, defending or helping others are especially suitable. These include Conrad, meaning 'wise counsellor', Alexander, 'defender of men', Dempster, 'wise judge', and Justin, 'just, fair'. And because Libra is all about weighing up opposing forces and being able to see both sides of an argument, names indicating a crossing, or a ford – places at which to change from one side to another – are likewise appropriate, including the obvious Ford as well as Lane, meaning 'passageway' and Travis, 'toll keeper'.

Finally, if you are looking for a good solid, fairly conservative name, Libra has plenty of these as well, including Alfred, 'good counsel', and David, 'beloved', for the boys, or Edna, 'pleasure, perfect happiness', and Grace, 'elegance, grace', for the girls.

100 Names for **Libra** Girls

A
Aki autumn
Alexandra/Alessia/Alexis defender of men
Amanda lovable
Ann/Anna/Anne favoured, grace
Annabel/Annabella beautiful Ann
Anneka alternative form of Ann
Annette/Annie little Ann
Anouska/Anushka alternative form of Ann
Anthea flowery
Anya alternative form of Ann
Aphrodite goddess of love (Venus)
Arabella alternative form of Annabella
Arleen/Arlene pledge
Autumn autumn
Aveline pleasantness
Azura blue

B
Belinda beautiful
Beryl gemstone (of Venus)
Bonnie/Bonny pretty

C
Callista of great beauty
Casimira bearer of peace
Charis/Charisa giver of graciousness
Charmaine charm, song
Cherie/Cherry/Sheree/Sheri sweet darling
Cheryl/Cheryll/Sheryl alternative forms of Cherie
Colinette little dove
Colleen girl
Columbine flower (of Venus)
Concordia harmony, concord
Cordelia harmony
Cosima harmony, order, beauty
Cyane blue

D
Damaris gentle
Danica morning star
Davina beloved, darling
Delicia delicate, pleasant
Delilah/Delinda/Delizea delight
Desideria/Desirée desirable
Dulcie sweet
Dysis sunset

E
Edna pleasure, perfect happiness
Erianthe sweetness, many flowers
Estelle/Esther/Stella morning star (Venus)

F
Florian flowery
Freda diminutive of Winifred
Frederica peaceful ruler
Freya goddess of love, beauty

G
Grace elegance, grace
Guinevere fair, beautiful wife
Gwendydd morning star

H
Hannah/Hanna favoured, grace
Harmonia harmony, unity

I
Imelda moderate
Inga/Ingrid fair, beautiful, fertile
Irene messenger of peace
Isadora/Isidora gift of Isis
Ishtar earlier (Assyrian) Venus

Sensitive Agreeable **Artistic**

J

Jemima dove
Jennifer alternative form of Guinevere
Jenny diminutive of Jennifer
Julia/Julie/Juliet downy-faced
Justina just, fair

L

Lentula mild
Linda/Lynda pretty, neat
Livia alternative form of Olivia
Lynette alternative form of Linda

M

Mabel lovely
Madeleine/Magdalen alternative forms of Magdalene
Madge/Maddie/Magda diminutives of Magdalene
Madlin/Madlyn/Madoline alternative forms of Magdalene
Magdalene woman of Magdala, Mary Magdalene
Malinda/Malina gentle
Mandy diminutive of Amanda
Marlene alternative form of Magdalene
Meline gentle
Melody singer of songs
Mirabel/Mirabella/Mirabelle great beauty
Miranda admirable
Moira gentle

N

Nancy/Nanette alternative forms of Ann
Naomi my delight
Nerine sea born (Venus)

O

Olive/Olivia peace

P

Pacifica peaceful
Pamela very sweet, lovely
Peace peace, happiness
Placida calm
Portia Shakespearean heroine (of justice), safe harbour
Prunella plant (of Venus)

R

Rebecca peacemaker, beauty

S

Sandra diminutive of Alexandra
Sapphire gemstone (of Venus)
Sasha diminutive of Alexandra
Serena calm, serene
Shirleen sweet
Shirley bright meadow, sweet
Sorrel herb (of Venus)

T

Tansy herb (of Venus)
Tegan/Tegwen beautiful, blessed
Themis goddess of justice and order

V

Vanessa butterfly
Venus goddess of love, beauty
Viola alternative form of Violet
Violante/Violetta alternative forms of Violet
Violet flower (of Venus), modesty
Violette little Violet

W

Winifred friend of peace

100 Names for **Libra** Boys

A

Adelfrid noble, peaceful
Adonis of manly beauty
Alan/Allan/Allen/Alun concord, rock
Alanus harmonious, cheerful
Alasdair/Alastair/Alister alternative forms of Alexander
Aleck/Alex/Alexis/Alick diminutives of Alexander
Alexander defender of men
Alfred good counsel, good advisor
Angwyn handsome
Asher evening

B

Beau handsome
Bellamy beautiful friend
Bentley from the winding, grassy meadow
Boydell wise fair one
Bradley dweller in the broad meadow

C

Cato sagacious
Cavanagh/Cavanaugh handsome
Chauncey chancellor, academic
Clark/Clarke charmer, learned man, clergyman
Clement merciful, mild
Clive statesman
Colin dove
Colman dove
Columba/Columbia/Columbus dove
Conrad wise counsellor, bold
Conway taking a wise course
Corwin heart's friend
Crosby dweller by the crossing
Culver dove

D

Dafydd alternative form of David
Daley/Daly assembly
Dan judge, law giver
Daniel my judge is God
Darrell/Daryl darling
Darren darling
Dave/Davey diminutives of David
David beloved
Dempster wise judge

E

Eros love god

F

Ferdinand peace, readiness
Finnegan fair, handsome
Florean flower beauty
Ford crossing
Fritz peaceful ruler

G

Gareth/Garth gentle
Gerwyn fair love
Gilbert bright pledge
Godfrey peace of god

H

Hassan handsome
Hendry manly
Humphrey supporting peace, protector

I

Isa equal

Sensitive Agreeable Artistic

J

Jefferson son of peace
Jeffrey/Geoffrey peaceful ruler
Jules diminutive of Julian
Julian/Julias soft-haired, downy-bearded
Justin just, fair
Justus alternative form of Justin

K

Kenneth handsome
Kevin handsome

L

Lane passageway
Lawton man of refinement
Lea/Lee/Leigh meadow
Leighton dweller in the herb garden
Lindo handsome
Linfred gentle grace
Lovelace love token

M

Malcolm devotee of the dove
Mallard strong in counsel
Manfred man of peace
Maxim premise, rule or guide
Miles grace, mild
Myron fragrant

N

Neal/Neil/Niall champion
Netis trusted friend

O

Oliver signifying peace
Otis keen of hearing

P

Philemon kiss, loving
Philo love

R

Ramon/Raymond protecting judge
Raynauld/Reynold well-counselled judgement
Rees ardour
Reeve/Reeves high official
Renard of firm decision
Renfred wise, peaceful judgement
Romeo romantic lover, pilgrim

S

Sandford sandy ford or crossing
Sandor/Sandy alternative forms of Alexander
Sanfred peaceful counsel
Scholem peace
Siegfried victorious peace
Solomon man of peace, wise
Stanford stony crossing

T

Terence tender, gracious
Travis toll keeper, crossroads, uniting

V

Valentine healthy, associated with romance

W

Wade meadow
Wesley/Westley of the west meadow
Wilfred resolute peace

Z

Zadoc just

Scorpio

ᛗ (The Scorpion)

24 October to **22 November**

Scorpio is intense – there is no escaping it. Have you ever looked at a Scorpio in a jealous rage and said something like, 'Come on, it's not a matter of life and death?' Oh dear – don't you realize that for Scorpio *everything* is a matter of life and death? These things have to be respected. It is this intensity and single-mindedness (also the origins of their legendary powers of perception and intuition) that can lead Scorpios to the heights of achievement in their chosen field. At the same time, they also like to dig deep and really get beneath the surface of everything they encounter in life's adventure. Strong in both body and spirit, they make loyal friends, passionate lovers (as any Scorpio will assure you) and conscientious workers. These are not people to mess with, but if you gain their respect, they are the very best people to have on your side in a crisis. And yes, they really do have a sense of humour – sometimes.

Ruling Planet

Traditionally Scorpio is ruled by Mars, signifying power, adventure, strength and aggression. Modern astrologers, however, often assign to Scorpio the more recently discovered Pluto, adding a mysterious though equally volatile ingredient to the already passionate Scorpio nature – for Pluto rules the underworld.

Element

Scorpio is a Fixed, Water sign, signifying extraordinary depth, like a great ocean or lake that is fathomless – qualities that resonate perfectly with the Scorpio love of the unseen and the mysterious.

Physical Characteristics

The body matches the spirit in being strong and sturdy. The boys are often compact in form and have a charismatic appeal, while the girls can be very attractive, giving rise to the legendary magnetism that those born under this sign seem to possess.

Health

Scorpio is robust and able to throw off illnesses quickly. However, the organs of elimination and reproduction are sometimes more susceptible than most to infections and disease. The emotions of jealousy and bitterness can cause nervous complaints if bottled up.

Famous Scorpios

Pablo Picasso
(Artist, born 25 October 1881)

John Cleese
(Comedian, born 27 October 1939)

Bill Gates
(Entrepreneur, born 28 October 1955)

Katherine Hepburn
(Actress, born 9 November 1909)

Demi Moore
(Actress, born 11 November 1962)

Leonardo DiCaprio
(Actor, born 11 November 1974)

Claude Monet
(Artist, born 14 November 1840)

Rock Hudson
(Actor, born 17 November 1925)

Lucky Connections

Gemstones	Colours	Plants	Metal
diamond	red	thistle	iron
garnet	saffron	nettle	steel
jasper		red rose	
ruby		poppy	

Raising a **Scorpio** Child

If you already have a Scorpio child, or one on the way, you will need to consider safety and security above all else – that is, *your* safety and security, not necessarily the baby's! Scorpios are nothing if not demonstrative, and they do enjoy pushing out the boundaries of discipline and good taste. Expect things to fly. The volatile and passionate nature of Scorpio is augmented, moreover, by an iron will, which makes them formidable opponents at any age. But the respect that grows out of adversity is an enduring quality, and they become loyal and very loving to those who stand their ground. Respect is, therefore, the key to understanding these intense little beings. They need space and privacy at home in order to concentrate and delve into the depths of their own thoughts and wishes – because they have their own unique way of making sense of the world, and can come up with some astonishing discoveries. They really are gifted – if given the chance. But always remember that emotion rules them. Humour versus sarcasm, kindness versus jealousy: their world is full of paradoxes and opposites that only they can reconcile.

Scorpio in the family home

Powerful and strong, Scorpio babies are determined little creatures and you will need a sturdy playpen or harness to contain them. Even then, you will have to be on your toes, because they are incurably partial to delving into places that should be out of bounds. Later, this will manifest itself in all manner of positive and progressive characteristics, making Scorpios the scientists or brave soldiers of tomorrow, but for now they will value a logical explanation or some straight talking when they overstep the mark. They are prone to jealousy, but are also very protective of siblings. They usually enjoy the company of their fellow Water signs, Pisces and Cancer, best of all, but also get on quite well with Virgo and Capricorn.

Friendship

To keep a Scorpio on board, friends simply have to be loyal and respectful. The Martial temperament of this sign insists on proper boundaries and protocols – and if anybody should dare to tread on the Scorpio tail, it will sting! There can be bitter recriminations or tearful tantrums, and it may take a long while to forget the pain – especially of rejection. As teenagers they become preoccupied with romance, and no less intense in this respect.

School

At school, Scorpio children are drawn to subjects that involve an element of mystery or discovery such as mathematics, science, geography or history. With a wisdom that is beyond their years, they can – and often do – discuss their ideas and questions in depth with their teachers and can become exemplary students, proud of both their school uniform and name. The famed physical prowess of Scorpio, along with a pretty powerful competitive spirit and sense of adventure, means that they usually enjoy sporting activities or martial arts, and can become central figures in all manner of other school pursuits.

Hobbies and interests

Scorpios often have secret hobbies, or at least like to have some kind of personal space in which to keep their favourite things away from prying eyes. There is nothing sinister at all about this – it is just their way, because they become intensely involved in whatever they undertake, be it a chemistry set or computer game. Considering the Martian affinity with steel, they might also enjoy activities that require the use of fine tools or machinery with which they can be wonderfully dextrous and skilful.

Choosing a Name for **Scorpio**

In choosing a name for a Scorpio child, we need to bear in mind the ideas of energy and intensity, along with the martial qualities of competitiveness and strength that Scorpio typifies. This leads us to some of the great classical names in the English language, such as Alexander or Alexandra, meaning 'defender of men', along with their many derivatives including Alex, Alexis, Alasdair, Sandy and Sandra. Then there is Andrew, derived from the Greek Andreas, meaning 'manly', which also provides us with the feminine derivative Andrea. And who can ignore the formidable Bernard, William and Herman for the boys, or the equally powerful Louisa, Martina or Bridget for the girls? All these names reflect the deep, often hidden strength of Scorpio.

Any name referring to the sting in the Scorpio tail is particularly apt: the traditional Hildegard, for instance, refers to a warrior maiden. Or there is the redoubtable Judith, meaning the 'avenging woman of Judea' who, in the Bible, wreaked revenge on the enemies of her people in typical Scorpio fashion – and from which we have the popular modern derivative Jodie.

But Scorpio is not just raw energy. Its Mars-like qualities are far more channelled and focused than in its Aries cousin, for example, and if you want to explore the Scorpio symbolism a little deeper, you need to look to the skies. There are two particularly bright stars in the night sky whose names can easily be associated with Scorpio: one, in the constellation of the Scorpion itself, the bright Antares, is a female name; the other, in the constellation of the eagle, Altair, is male. The eagle is an important symbol for Scorpio which, along with the serpent, has been applied to this sign over the centuries. These are far more positive symbols, and provide us with a more acceptable and broader-based personality for the Scorpio individual – a being who can soar to the heights or explore the depths of wisdom, like the eagle and the serpent respectively. Names referring to these creatures include Belinda, meaning 'sinuous, serpent-like', or the Teutonic Arnold, Adelar and Arno, all boys' names that refer to the eagle.

But Scorpio goes even deeper than this. In mythology, and in the astrological symbolism that draws so heavily upon it, we meet with the mysterious and enduring legend of Demeter, goddess of the harvest, and her daughter Kore who is associated with the temporary suspension of life during winter. Kore was kept in the underworld for the winter months, and then released by Pluto and returned to the world to bring forth renewed life each spring. This wonderful, mysterious story (which is also encountered in connection with the star sign Virgo) has a strong resonance with the intense Scorpio character, so names such as Cora, or Kore itself, the 'maiden who returns', are suitable choices, along with her flower, the Poppy.

Remaining with the world of the unseen, Scorpio has always been considered a magical sign. Names hinting at magic and sorcery are therefore also to be found in our list, especially female names like Camille, the sorceress from Arthurian legend, or the very modern creation Samantha, the kindly witch popularized in the well-known 1960s television series *Bewitched*. All new life has a magical side to it, of course – sometimes playful, sometimes inspirational – but with Scorpio we meet this reality head-on.

100 Names for **Scorpio** Girls

A

Acantha thorny
Alexandra defender of men
Alexis alternative form of Alexander
Alison war maid
Alphonsine ready for combat
Amalia/Amelia eager, striving
Andrea brave
Antares bright star (in Scorpio)
Ardelia/Ardis/Ardra ardent, zealous
Arlette eagle
Arnhilda battle maid
Astrid godly strength
Athena/Athene warrior goddess of wisdom

B

Belinda sinuous, serpent-like
Berenice/Bernice bringer of victory
Bernadette little maid, brave as a bear
Bernadine bold, masterful
Bernessa valorous, bear-like
Bernette alternative form of Bernadette
Bramble thorny bush
Brenda flaming sword
Briana strong, fearless
Briar thorny, wild rose bush
Bridget/Brigitte/Brigitta strength
Briony/Bryony herb (of Mars)
Bronya armour

C

Camille Arthurian sorceress
Carletta little virile one
Cassandra exciting love, prophetess
Colette alternative form of Nicola
Cora alternative form of Kore

D

Deirdre/Deidra/Deidre tempestuous
Delilah/Delinda alluring, delight
Desirée desired
Diadema diadem
Diamanta of diamonds
Diamond gemstone (of Mars)
Dyna power

E

Edith successful warrior maid
Emily rival, eager
Enid soul
Ernestine serious, earnest
Eunice good victory
Eva/Eve life, temptress

F

Faith powerful trust

G

Geralda courageous
Geraldine powerful contender, spear rule
Gerda girdled, warrior maid
Gertrude spear maid
Giralda powerful contender
Griselda indomitable maid
Gudrun god's secret

H

Hedda/Hedy contention
Hedwig alternative form of Hedda
Hilda/Hildegard battle maid

Intense Intuitive Steadfast

I

Isa spirit of iron

J

Jodie/Jody/Judy diminutives of Judith
Judith woman of Judea, avenging

K

Kalwa heroic
Kim/Kimberley place of diamonds
Kore maiden of the underworld

L

Lara alternative form of Laura
Laura victorious
Laurissa alternative form of Laura
Leda beautiful temptress
Lexia diminutive of Alexander
Lora/Lorella alternative forms of Laura
Loren/Lorraine alternative forms of Laura
Louella shrewd battle maid
Louisa/Louise famous battle maid

M

Marcella/Marcia/Marsha alternative forms of Martina
Martina brave, of Mars
Matilda warrior maid
Maud alternative form of Matilda
Medea enchantress, ruler
Mena mercy, strength
Mimi resolute opponent
Minerva warrior goddess of wisdom

N

Nicola/Nicole victorious

P

Pallas wise warrior maiden
Phoenix blood red, rising again
Poppy flower of remembrance

R

Renita resistance
Rita brave, honest
Romilda brave little battle maid
Ruby gemstone (of Mars)

S

Samantha sorceress (modern usage)
Sandra diminutive of Alexandra
Scarlett dyer of red cloth
Seraphina ardent
Sibyl/Sybil wise woman, prophetess
Sigrid beauty, victory
Sonia alternative form of Sophia
Sophia/Sophie/Sophy wisdom
Storm stormy, tempestuous

T

Terry powerful tribe
Tilda/Tillie/Tilly diminutive of Matilda
Tina diminutive of Martina

V

Valda spirited, power
Valencia strong
Valentina/Valentine strong and valorous one
Valerie to be strong

W

Wilma/Wylma resolute contender

100 Names for **Scorpio** Boy

A

Abelard of noble firmness
Adelar/Adlar noble eagle
Ahrens power of the eagle
Alasdair/Alastair/Alister alternative forms of Alexander
Alec/Alex/Alexis diminutives of Alexander
Alexander defender of men
Altair bright star in Aquila (eagle)
Andreas alternative form of Andrew
Andrew manly, brave
Andy diminutive of Andrew
Archibald very bold
Arden/Ardin fervent, ardent
Ares Mars, god of war
Ari eagle
Arno eagle
Arnold eagle rule
Arnvid eagle of the forest

B

Balin soldier of distinction
Banister wild pomegranate
Barry direct, spearhead
Baynard reddish brown
Bernard hardy, bold, bear-like
Bill/Billy diminutives of William

C

Cadfael battle metal
Cador shield
Caesar to cut
Calvin bold
Cavell active and bold
Cledwyn blessed sword
Colin people's victory
Connor examiner
Conway he who takes a wise course

D

Darwin courageous friend
Drew (from Andrew) skilled in magic
Driscoll thicket of wild roses
Durand/Durant endurance, lasting
Durwood unflinching guard

E

Egmont sword protector, patriot
Emlyn rival
Erhard intelligent resolution
Ernest/Earnest/Ernie serious, earnest
Ernst alternative form of Ernest

F

Fergus strong, man of vigour
Ferris man of iron
Fortescue strong shield

G

Garner protecting warrior
Gavin/Gawain hawk of battle
Gideon hewer
Gruffydd strong warrior

H

Harold champion, general
Harry diminutive of Harold
Hector to hold fast, firm
Herman/Hermann soldier, warrior
Humphrey peaceful warrior
Huya fighting eagle

I

Igor hero
Isard tough as iron

Intense Intuitive Steadfast

J
Jarratt firm combatant
Jerwais armed for battle

K
Keenan sharp
Kenway valiant soldier

L
Lewis/Louis famous warrior
Liam alternative form of William

M
Marcius/Marcus martial
Marius alternative form of Mark
Mark warrior, of Mars
Marsden valley of combat
Martel war hammer
Martin of Mars
Marvin warrior friend
Maska powerful
Medwin strong, worthy companion

N
Nial/Niall/Nils champion
Nicander man of victory
Nico alternative form of Nicander

P
Paco bold eagle

R
Ragmar wise warrior
Rainer prudent warrior
Randall/Randolph edge of shield, wolf
Ravelin rampart
Rawdon red roe
Raymond protecting advisor
Rayner/Raynor advising, discreet warrior
Read/Reade ruddy
Reece/Rees ardour
Reginald advising ruler
Roy/Rory red

S
Sandy alternative form of Alexander
Saxon short-sword warrior
Searle/Searles/Serlo wearer of armour
Sheldon shield bearer
Siegfried peaceful victory
Sloane warrior

T
Tabor fortified encampment

V
Valdis spirited warrior
Valentine strong, valorous one, romance
Victor victorious
Vincent conquering

W
Walter military leader
Ward one who keeps guard
William helmet of will, defender
Wilhelm/Willard alternative forms of William
Wilmot alternative form of William

Sagittarius

♐ (The Archer)

23 November to 21 December

Sagittarius is the zodiac's great marksman – but what exactly is it aiming at? Every Sagittarian, in their own typically jovial and cheerful way, will probably give you a different answer, but aiming at something they surely are – something distant and idealistic, perhaps, or maybe just at having a good time and enjoying all the rich variety that life has to offer. Whatever it is, Sagittarius, with its larger-than-life attitude, will go to enormous lengths to hit the mark – and distance is no object. Sagittarians can travel the globe, learn a dozen languages and study for years to achieve their goal – and, in the process, discover and pass on considerable wisdom and learning to their fellow men and women. Sincere, playful and yet thoughtful, too, these are the ideas people of the zodiac – big ideas, too, and plenty of them, with hearts to match.

Ruling Planet

Sagittarius is ruled by the expansive, philosophical Jupiter. The bringer of joy, Jupiter is a planet that protects and preserves – bestowing a larger-than-life touch to everything, including people. It relates to ideas, education and the law.

Element

Belonging to the Fire element, Sagittarius is also a Mutable sign. Warm-hearted and fiery, this combination is capable of great achievement, and able to adapt and change at will to suit unfamiliar circumstances. It inclines to travel and exploration of all kinds.

Physical Characteristics

Sagittarians often have a fleshy, rounded, jovial appearance. Their eyes seem to be smiling much of the time, like the sun appearing from behind clouds. The thighs are often strong.

Health

Traditionally, Sagittarius is said to rule the buttocks and thighs. Health is usually very robust and hearty, but Sagittarius does everything on a large scale and can over-indulge, sometimes leading to weight problems or toxicity of the blood.

Famous Sagittarians

Harpo Marx
(Comic actor, born 23 November 1888)

Scott Joplin
(Jazz composer, born 24 November 1868)

Billy Connolly
(Comedian, born 24 November 1942)

Tina Turner
(Singer, born 26 November 1939)

Jimi Hendrix
(Musician, born 27 November 1942)

Winston Churchill
(Statesman, born 30 November 1874)

Walt Disney
(Film-maker, born 5 December 1901)

Kim Basinger
(Actress, born 8 December 1953)

Lucky Connections

Gemstones	Colours	Plants	Metal
emerald	green	acanthus	tin
jade	blue	borage	
amethyst	purple	fig	
		oak	

Raising a **Sagittarius** Child

Are you good at answering questions? You will certainly get plenty of practice if you have a little Sagittarian on the way, because their curiosity is such that they simply never stop. They wake up in the morning with a question on their lips and fall asleep in the afternoon half-way through another. Life is one big adventure, a hill to climb, from which – Sagittarius always hopes – the full vista of life will be revealed. They love animals, and revel in play-acting of all kinds. Above all, Sagittarians are honest. Whatever is on their mind just pops out, regardless of who might be in the way, but it's all done with such innocence and joviality that no one really minds. In fact, joviality is what Sagittarius is all about – the word itself comes from the sign's ruling planet, Jupiter. These playful little clowns will keep you amused forever with their jokes and quirky observations. Sure, they do tend to be a little clumsy at times, and to invite their pets and animals with muddy paws into the bedroom – but they won't change, and you really wouldn't want them to, would you?

Sagittarius in the family home

If you have a Sagittarian about the house, you will automatically have to make room for some pets as well. Ideally, these would include a horse or two and several dogs, but even after suitable scaling down, at least a few furry creatures of some description will be essential companions to growing Sagittarians – they simply love them! Don't worry, they like people, too, and enjoy the company of anyone who shares their sense of adventure and wonder. In this, they get on best with their fellow Fire signs, Leo and Aries, but also quite well with two of the Air signs, Libra and Aquarius.

Friendship

Friends for Sagittarians must be honest and sincere individuals. They have no time for cheats or liars, or even those who are over-diplomatic or cautious. After all, *they* shoot from the hip, so why shouldn't everybody else? 'Loosen up a little' is the Sagittarian cry – perhaps they are right. They enjoy people with wit and intelligence, therefore, ideally with both qualities combined in equal measure. They also love a good party, with lots of fun and games – the bigger and the merrier, the better! Keep the tin hat handy!

School

Not easy to discipline, Sagittarians respond best if given logical explanations. Providing their teachers can ignite their fiery little spirit and inspire them, they will study hard and feel at ease with even the most intractable of subjects. They enjoy rough-and-tumble sports where they can bulldoze their way to glory, but are also attracted towards subjects that feed the spirit, such as philosophy or religious studies. Quite a combination – but it is precisely this boisterous attitude to learning that can drive them on to become the great academics of life.

Hobbies and interests

Sagittarius children like to feed their sense of adventure through lots of outings – discovering different places and people. They love travel, and holidays will be eagerly anticipated. What's more, you may find they learn all those foreign languages with such ease that they quickly become the official translator of the party. Sagittarians adore animals and pets, too, and the girls will want to ride horses, the boys to run and skip with their dogs. Their sunny nature attracts them to artistic pursuits, but there will also be interests in the fields of law, the military, politics and religion.

Choosing a Name for **Sagittarius**

With its pictogram of an archer mounted on a horse (some say it is a centaur: half-horse, half-man), Sagittarius naturally produces its fair share of animal lovers. In this context, the names Philip or Philippa, meaning 'lover of horses', make highly suitable choices. The Teutonic root for the word horse – ross – gives rise to several popular female names such as Rosamund, Rosalind and, some say, Rose as well.

However, it is the bright, optimistic and effusive Jupiter, ruling planet of Sagittarius, that provides the key to many of the names included in our lists. It is interesting to note just how many female names start with the letter J, derived in part from the term jovial, itself derived from Jupiter. Thus we have Jocelyn, Jovita, Joy, Joyleen and more.

Jupiter is the Roman name for the earlier Greek Zeus, the chief of the pantheon of all the Olympian gods and mythological heroes of ancient times – a figure which also finds a resonance in the Teutonic Wodin or Odin. So, as well as joviality we are also looking at power, energy, abundance and potent spirit here. The Olympians supplanted the older gods, the Titans, and from this evolution came all the benefits that we mortals are said to enjoy: laws, customs, the very fabric of civilization. With time, this process was repeated over and over again, with one culture supplanting another – giving rise to names such as Jacob and Jacques, meaning 'supplanter', and from which we derive James and Jacqueline and their many derivatives, including Jim and Jackie. Some scholars insist that Jack stems from the name John, others that it comes from the French Jacques: both these sources are to be found in our lists.

Ultimately, Sagittarians always strive to broaden their horizons, no matter how. Throughout the ages, the two great Sagittarian passions of travel and ideas (including religious and spiritual ideas) have become embodied in the figure of the pilgrim, the wandering sage, so we can choose some unusual names such as Wendelin, 'wanderer', and Peregrine or Palmer, both meaning 'pilgrim'. Because the concept of faith in general must be placed under the rulership of this potentially most spiritual of signs, you will find here two of our most beautiful and enduring of names. For the girls, there is Elizabeth, meaning 'God's oath', and its many derivatives such as Elise and Elspeth. For the boys, there is John, meaning 'God has favoured, grace of God', along with its many derivatives including Ian and Shawn.

Meanwhile, the hawk or eagle – the noble and fierce creature invariably associated with the leading deity of any pantheon – provides us with Arabella, 'beautiful eagle' and Gavin, 'hawk of battle'. Further emblems, such as the spear or the cornucopia (horn of plenty) associated with Zeus and Odin and which relate well to the larger-than-life quality of this sign, can be discovered in names such as Cornelius, 'horn-like', or Edgar, 'rich spear'. The bow and arrow of Sagittarius, made from the yew tree, provide further names, including Ivor, meaning 'archer, bowman', or Archibald, 'bold archer', for the boys, and the delightful Yvette or Yvonne for the girls, and which again stem from the word 'yew'.

Finally, because Jupiter has always been considered the planet of preservation and protection, we can also include names such as Edmond, 'defender of property', and Hera, the 'goddess protector of women and marriage'.

100 Names for **Sagittarius** Girls

A

Abbie diminutive of Abigail
Abigail my father rejoices, joy
Adione traveller's friend
Alethea truth
Ann/Anne/Anna grace
Annabel/Annabella beautiful Ann
Anita alternative form of Ann
Anouska alternative form of Ann
Aquila eagle
Aquilina little eagle
Arabella beautiful eagle
Ariadne/Arianna to delight, beautiful
Ashley ash wood

B

Babs diminutive of Barbara
Barbara foreign woman, stranger
Beatrice/Beatrix blessed, joyful, voyager

C

Carla/Carrie alternative forms of Caroline
Carol/Carole alternative forms of Caroline
Caroline/Carolina/Carolyn free
Charity charity, kind giver
Charlotte alternative form of Caroline
Cornelia horn-like (cornucopia)

D

Dacia from afar
Danielle God is my judge
Daria one who has knowledge
Dilys genuine
Dora/Dorea alternative forms of Theodora
Doreen/Dorena/Dorinda alternative forms of Theodora
Dorothea/Dorothy alternative forms of Theodora

E

Edana/Edna alternative forms of Edith
Edeva alternative form of Edith
Edith happy, cheerful
Elise/Elli alternative forms of Elizabeth
Elizabeth oath of God
Elsa/Elsie/Elspeth alternative forms of Elizabeth
Emerald gemstone (of Jupiter)
Emma whole, universal
Esmerelda emerald

F

Felicity luck, opportune
Felipa alternative form of Philippa
Fortuna goddess of fortune
Frances free, from France
Fronia thinker

G

Gelasia laughing girl
Geraldine spear ruler
Gypsy wanderer, traveller

H

Helga happy, holy, healing
Hera goddess protector of women and marriage
Hilary cheerful, merry
Honesta honourable, honest
Honor integrity, honour
Hope optimistic, trusting
Hyacinth royal purple flower, sapphire

I

Ida happy
Isabel/Isabella/Isobel alternative forms of Elizabeth

Optimistic Spontaneous **Adventurous**

J

Jacinta/Jacinth/Jacintha wearer of the purple
Jackie diminutive of Jacqueline
Jacqueline supplanter
Jade green semi-precious stone
Jane God has favoured, grace of God
Janet little one of divine grace
Jean alternative form of Jane
Jessica/Jessie alternative forms of Janet
Joan grace of God, God has favoured
Joanna/Johanna alternative forms of Joan
Jocelin/Jocelyn playful
Jocunda mirthful
Jodette sporting
Jodis horse sprite
Jofrid lover of horses
Joletta violet, flower (of Jupiter)
Jorna traveller
Joscelind gentle playmate
Jovita jovial
Joy/Joya/Joyan/Joyce pleasure, rejoicing
Joyleen alternative form of Joy
Joyvita jovial, merry
Juno goddess, wife of Jupiter

K

Kelley/Kelly from 'church'
Kendra woman of knowledge, understanding
Kyla/Kylie alternative forms of Kelley

L

Letitia/Leta/Lettice gladness, joy
Linnet/Lynette shapely

M

Mabel alternative form of Annabel
Miriam exalted

N

Nadine hope
Nora/Norah honourable

O

Olga alternative form of Helga
Olympia of Olympus, high, heavenly

P

Petula seeker
Phenice of the stately palm tree
Philippa/Pippa lover of horses

R

Rayma rambler
Rita honest, brave
Rosalind tender horse
Rosamund horse protection

S

Sian alternative form of Jane

T

Theodora bountiful, gift from God

V

Vera truth, faith
Verona truthful

W

Wendelin wanderer

Y

Yvette from 'yew', grace of the Lord
Yvonne alternative form of Yvette

Z

Zina from Zeus

100 Names for **Sagittarius** Boy

A

Ahearn/Ahern lord of the horses
Ahrens power of the eagle
Archer bowman, archer
Archibald bold archer
Ashley/Ashleigh ash wood

B

Barry direct, spearhead
Bonar good
Boniface doing of good, benefactor

C

Calvin bold
Carl alternative form of Charles
Cato sagacious
Chae/Chas/Chaz diminutives of Charles
Charles/Charlie free man
Charlton alternative form of Charles
Clarence illustrious
Connell wise chief
Cornelius horn-like (cornucopia)
Cuthbert brilliant wisdom, splendour

D

Damian/Damon to subdue or tame
Daniel my judge is God
Darius wealthy preserver
Delvin a pilgrim
Dermot father of oaks
Dewar pilgrim
Dipak/Deepak light, little lamp

E

Edgar rich spear
Edmund defender of property
Elias cheerful
Eliot/Elliot/Elliott God's own given one
Elisha God is generous, my salvation
Ellis (from Elisha) benevolent
Elmo amiable
Elmore the greater
Elwin/Elwyn godly friend
Emanuel/Emmanuel God is with us
Emery strong, powerful, wealthy
Erastus amiable
Errol wandering
Esmond protected by the gods
Euan/Ewan/Ewen from 'yew'

F

Falkner/Faulkner trainer of hawks
Fletcher maker of arrows
Francis free, from France
Franklin/Franklyn free man
Frayne ash tree (of Odin)

G

Galahad knight
Garner protecting warrior
Garvey spear bearer
Gavin hawk of battle
Gerald/Gerard/Gerhard strong with a spear
Gerry diminutive of Gerald
Gervaise servant of the spear
Gifford brave giver

Optimistic Spontaneous **Adventurous**

H

Hamish alternative form of James
Hank/Hanke alternative forms of John
Hubbard mindful, thinker
Hubert bright, mindful
Hugh/Hew/Hugo mindful, thinker
Humbert bright giant
Humphrey protector of the home
Hunter huntsman
Huya fighting eagle

I

Ian/Iain alternative forms of John
Illaris merry
Isaac laughter
Isaiah the Lord is his salvation
Ivor archer, bowman

J

Jack/Jake alternative forms of James
Jacob supplanter
Jacques alternative form of James
James supplanter
Jeremy/Jerry exalted of God
Jim diminutive of James
Johan/Johann alternative forms of John
John God has favoured, grace of God
Jovian of Jupiter

K

Kirk house of worship, church
Kirkland dweller on church land

L

Latimer interpreter
Lorimer maker of bridles
Loy open

M

Macaire happy
Manuel alternative form of Emanuel

O

Ormond famous protector
Oscar godly spear
Owen alternative form of Euan

P

Palmer pilgrim to the holy land
Peregrine pilgrim, traveller
Philip lover of horses

R

Rama bringer of joy
Richmond protecting ruler
Rodger/Roger praise
Romero wanderer
Ross horse

S

Salvador saviour
Seamus/Shamus alternative forms of James
Sean/Shane/Shaun/Shawn alternative forms of John
Shanahan sagacious, wise

T

Thaddeus wise, praise

W

Wendell wanderer

Y

Yve/Yves alternative forms of Ivor

Capricorn

♑ (The Goat)

22 December to **20 January**

Steady, dependable, with a natural air of authority about them, Capricorns seem to take life pretty seriously a lot of the time – if not actually *all* of the time! These are the leaders, the entrepreneurs and captains of industry – the people who make things work. They are happiest if there is a goal in sight, an ambition to be realized, and are capable of designing the most intricate and far-reaching of plans in order to achieve their ends. Without being flashy or drawing attention to themselves, Capricorns are life's real winners. Like the goat itself, climbing slowly from crag to crag, they reach the summit eventually, using skill and determination. Proud, dignified and clever, Capricorns are masters of irony and satire and yet, ultimately, they respect tradition – honouring their predecessors in whichever field they choose to work.

Ruling Planet

Capricorn is ruled by Saturn, the planet of seniority, age and wisdom. Saturn is also all about time, measurement, tradition and law. Slow, deliberate and powerful, Saturn bestows a natural air of maturity and authority.

Element

Capricorn belongs to the Earth element, and is Cardinal in nature. This pairing relates to leadership combined with prudence and caution. Ambition and responsibility are mixed to good effect here, along with ample supplies of common sense.

Physical Characteristics

With their swarthy complexions and wiry, sometimes slender figures, Capricorns have a mature, distinguished appearance that becomes very handsome with the passing years. The men can have prominent Adam's apples, and the women usually possess great style.

Health

Capricorn tends towards cold, rheumatic complaints rather than feverish illnesses. Traditionally, it is the joints and especially the knees that are the main areas of concern. Capricorn can also be melancholic.

Famous Capricorns

Ralph Fiennes
(Actor, born 22 December 1962)

Nigel Kennedy
(Violinist, born 28 December 1956)

Mel Gibson
(Actor, born 3 January 1956)

Joan Baez
(Singer, born 9 January 1941)

Rod Stewart
(Singer, born 10 January 1945)

Martin Luther King
(Civil rights leader, born 15 January 1929)

Kate Moss
(Model, born 16 January 1974)

Edgar Allan Poe
(Author, born 19 January 1809)

Lucky Connections

Gemstones	Colour	Plants	Metal
diamond	black	holly	lead
onyx		ivy	
obsidian		rue	
jet			

Raising a **Capricorn** Child

Don't worry if your Capricorn child is wearing a frown: he or she isn't necessarily unhappy, just thinking. Utterly focused on the issues of the moment, Capricorns are planning and wondering just how to go about getting their way – which they always do, of course, in the end. Expect a grown-up dialogue with your little goat, a mature discussion every once in a while about where to go or what to do. Capricorns like to be involved – in fact, they actually prefer being in charge, if you can bear it. They do respect authority, however, and if you can convince them that you know best, and that you will let them in on the secret of how you know, they will follow obediently. Above all, you can trust Capricorns. You can give them responsibilities and duties to perform, and if there is a reward attached to the task, they will jump to it. It's as good as done – if not exactly in a flash, then at least in the fullness of time … that is, *their* time (which may be quite a while). Be patient!

Capricorns in the family home

Capricorns love home – so much so, that it might be a job to get your little goat to exercise and take fresh air. The home is their empire, where they are masters of all they survey, and until the drive for worldly achievement kicks in they will be cautious about venturing forth. They prefer a quiet outing with their parents to roaming around with a gang (it's so much more dignified!). Sometimes shy, but usually quietly confident, they get on best with their fellow Earth signs, Taurus and Virgo, but also quite well with Scorpio and Pisces, and they sometimes develop a parental attitude to their siblings, even those who are older.

Friendship

In matters of friendship, Capricorn tends towards a few close playmates rather than lots of superficial contacts. A 'meeting of minds' is far more likely than a whirlwind infatuation, and friends must be sensible and mature. Often, the people they like are those who share common goals and ambitions. The few who are honoured in this way can become lifetime buddies and soulmates.

School

Well-behaved – most of the time – Capricorn children rarely get into trouble at school. Providing their ambitions can be activated they can work incredibly hard, taking full responsibility for homework and exams on their own broad shoulders. Proud by nature, they would never want to be seen to be 'letting the side down' in any sense. With their quiet, natural air of authority and sense of duty, Capricorns can also become successful representatives or leaders in class, though sports might not be too high on their list of priorities unless there are appropriate plaudits or honours to be had.

Hobbies and interests

Capricorns often become 'the authority' in their chosen field, and that includes hobbies, whether it be collecting stamps or building computers. In other words, if they can't take it seriously, it is probably not going to attract them at all. Expect some quirky interests along the way, such as fossils, stones and shells, clocks, family or local history, and even archaeology. Capricorn hobbies are definitely different.

Choosing a Name for **Capricorn**

In choosing a name for this most powerful and yet dignified of signs, we have to bear in mind the nature of its ruling planet, Saturn – the great Earth element embodied in the principles of caution, order and tradition. All those names which refer to these principles and to the noble, steadfast nature of Saturn are therefore suitable choices for our lists. So for the girls we have Sonia, meaning 'wisdom', or Norma, 'exact to a pattern or precept', and for the boys there is Brian, 'strong, dignified', and Richard, 'brave ruler'.

Saturn and Capricorn also relate to dark colours, and especially to black, and there are numerous names in the English language that refer to this, many beginning with the letter D. For the boys we have Douglas, meaning 'dark stream', Donahue, 'dark', and Donelly, 'dark man'. For the girls there is Maureen, again meaning 'dark', and Melanie, 'one in black'. Darkness in this context is not necessarily anything sinister, but rather signifies the great feminine principles symbolized by night, the starry sky, or the depth and mystery of the earth. Some rare and beautiful names come from these sources including Isra, 'nocturnal journey', and Hesper, 'night star', while the boys also have some unusual candidates, such as Kieran, meaning 'black', and Maurice, 'swarthy'.

The raven and blackbird, both dark or black in colour, have also been given their role in the creation of names such as Brenna, 'maiden with raven hair', Merle, 'blackbird', and Mervin, 'raven of the sea'. Still drawing on the natural world, we have Cole, 'black, as coal', for the boys and the delightful and mysterious Ebony, 'dark wood', for the girls.

Capricorn and Saturn also traditionally relate to broad, open spaces – heathland and lowland, along with barren, craggy hillsides (favourite terrain of the goat, of course), so you will find names such as Sharon, meaning 'the plain (also to sing)', or Craig, 'from the mountain crag', in the lists. The boys also have their fair share of names signifying power and leadership, particularly salient Capricorn features. In this context we have the formidable Dominic, meaning 'Lord', and the equally noteworthy Max or Maximilian, a name which quite unashamedly means 'greatest'. Feminine derivatives of this are Maxine or Maxie.

The sun enters the sign of Capricorn around 22 December, so names that refer to Christmas must automatically be considered when choosing a name for a child born at this time. Noel for the boys or Noella for the girls are obvious choices, but alternatives also include Natalie, 'Christmas child', and Leslie or Lesley, 'garden of hollies' – and we should not forget Holly itself, the simple choice often being the best. A modern favourite for the girls is Tiffany, thought to be derived from the word Epiphany, the festival of Twelfth Night, so again clearly related to Capricorn.

Time, its measurement and its passing are important to Capricorn, and the Latin-derived word 'hour' finds its resonance in names such as Horace and Horatio. In fact, all those names which can be associated with planning, measurement or order – and the authority needed to impose these on the otherwise chaotic universe – can be placed under Capricorn. Danella, meaning 'wise mistress', or Priscilla, 'old, longevity', are therefore suitable for the girls, along with Ernest, meaning just that – 'earnest', or Conan, 'high in wisdom', for the boys. Finally, Capricorn often has a fascination with shells, fossils, bones or stones of various kinds, so you will find names such as Coral for the girls and Dunstan, 'dark stone', for the boys.

100 Names for **Capricorn** Girls

A

Aenea praiseworthy
Almira the exalted one
Alysia unbroken bond
Amelia hardworking, industrious
Andrea brave
Anthelia opposite the Sun

B

Branwen/Brangwirin little raven
Brenna maiden with raven hair
Burnetta little brown one

C

Carissa dear little schemer
Cattima slender reed
Celeste heavenly
Celestina/Celestine alternative forms of Celeste
Ciara dark
Clarinita famous little one
Clarmond world-famed
Clearesta highest peak of glory
Cleine famous
Cleodorra glorious gift
Cleopatra from a famous father
Cleosa famous
Concha seashell
Coral coral
Cornelia horn-like

D

Danella wise mistress
Danette little mistress
Della noble
Dominique/Dominica mistress, lady

E

Earnestine earnest, serious
Ebony dark wood
Elda woman of noble family
Emily/Emilia rival, industrious
Erica ever ruler
Esme esteemed, loved

G

Germaine akin, belonging

H

Hesper night star
Holly plant (of Saturn), of Christmas
Honor/Honora/Honoria integrity, honour
Hypatia accomplished

I

Ines daughter
Irette little wrathful one
Isra nocturnal journey
Ivy clinging vine, constancy

K

Kay maker, keeper of keys
Kayley/Kayleigh alternative forms of Kay and Kelly
Kelly Irish surname, from church or strife
Kerry from county Kerry, dark
Kiara/Kiera/Keera/Kyara alternative forms of Ciara

L

Lalla of the lowlands
Lara diminutive of Larissa
Larissa famous citadel
Leila dark beauty, loyal, night
Lesley garden of hollies

Ambitious Commanding **Wise**

M

Martha lady
Maureen dark
Maurilla wise, dark-eyed girl
Maurita little dark girl
Maxine/Maxie/Maxy greatest
Medea she who rules
Melanie one in black
Melonia dark
Melva/Melvina chief
Meras worthy
Merle/Merula blackbird
Michaela she who is like a goddess
Mildred mild power
Minnie remembrance
Monica adviser

N

Natalie Christmas child
Natalya/Natasha alternative forms of Natalie
Nerys Lady
Nicky/Nikky diminutives of Nicola
Nicola/Nicole people's victory, Christmas
Nigella black
Noeleen alternative form of Noella
Noella/Noelle the nativity, of Christmas
Nora/Norah alternative forms of Honor
Norine honourable
Norma exact to a pattern or precept

O

Odelia heiress, prosperous

P

Patrice alternative form of Patricia
Patricia patrician, noble
Pattie/Patty diminutives of Patricia
Priscilla old, longevity
Prudence careful, prudence

R

Raven raven, black
Richelle brave ruler
Rue herb (of Saturn)

S

Sabina Sabine woman (ancient race)
Sabrina legendary daughter of English king
Sadie diminutive of Sara
Sally diminutive of Sara
Sara/Sarah princess
Savannah treeless plain
Shannon Irish river, the old one
Sharon the plain (also to sing)
Sonia alternative form of Sophia
Sophia/Sophie/Sophy wisdom

T

Tara hill, earth goddess
Tiffany from Epiphany, Twelfth Night
Trish/Trisha diminutives of Patricia

100 Names for **Capricorn** Boys

A

Aaron/Aron high mountain
Abbot head of the abbey, father
Abraham father of a multitude
Aldous old
Algernon bearded
Andrew manly, brave
Andros manly

B

Barnabus son of consolation
Barnaby alternative form of Barnabus
Bertram illustrious one, bright raven
Bran raven
Brian/Bryan strong, dignified
Brion nobly descended
Burnett brown

C

Clarendon famous gentleman
Clifton dweller by the cleft rock
Clint/Clinton settlement on the summit
Cole black, as coal
Coleridge dweller by the black ridge
Colley swarthy, black-haired
Conan high in wisdom
Corbet raven
Cornelius horn-like
Corvin raven, black
Craig from the mountain crag
Cyril lord and master

D

Darcy/D'Arcy dark
Desmond man of the world
Devereaux dutiful
Dick diminutive of Richard
Dietmar famous race of people
Dolan dark-haired
Dominic lord
Don diminutive of Donahue, Donald or Donovan
Donaghan of dark complexion
Donahue dark
Donald world mighty
Donelly dark man
Donovan dark warrior
Dougal dark stranger
Douglas dark stream
Doyle dark stranger
Drew diminutive of Andrew
Duane/Dwayne dark, black
Duff dark, black
Duke leader
Dunbar dark branch
Duncan dark battle
Dunstan dark stone

E

Earnst alternative form of Ernest
Eldred mature counsellor
Eldwin old friend
Emery powerful, rich
Eric ever ruler
Ernest/Earnest serious, earnest
Ethan firmness
Ewald always powerful

Ambitious Commanding **Wise**

G
Gemmel old
Giles young goat, shield
Gordon spacious hill fort
Graham dweller at the grey manor, stern
Grant tall man

H
Harding hardy, tough
Hardy alternative form of Harding
Hayward guardian/dweller by the ledge or dark forest
Haywood wood within the ledge
Heath high plain
Heyward dweller by the dark forest
Horace time
Horatio alternative form of Horace

I
Ingram raven

K
Kane/Kain dark
Kerrin/Kerryn alternative forms of Kieran
Kieran black
Kim chief

L
Lars lord
Leslie garden of hollies
Lloyd grey
Lombard long beard

M
Magnus great
Maurice/Morris Moorish, swarthy
Max diminutive of Maximilian
Maximilian greatest
Maxwell Magnus's stream
Melville/Melvin chief of the people
Merrick dark, swarthy
Mervin/Mervyn raven of the sea
Morrell dark, swarthy

N
Nero strong, stern
Nicholas people's victory, of Christmas
Nigel dark, black
Noah long rest, consolation
Noel/Nowell the nativity, of Christmas

O
Olaf/Olav/Olave ancestral relic, descendant

P
Packy/Paddy/Pat diminutives of Patrick
Patrick patrician, nobleman
Phineas black, swarthy, oracle

R
Ricardo/Rich/Richie/Rick alternative forms of Richard
Richard brave ruler, harsh king
Roddy/Rod alternative forms of Roderick
Roderick fame and power

S
Sidney wide land by the marsh

T
Timothy honour, respect, god-like
Titus honoured, titled, safe

Aquarius

♒ (The Water Carrier)

21 January to **19 February**

Sometimes it seems the versatile Aquarian brain was custom-built to cope with the endless distractions and information overload of the modern age. It roams from one item to another in the way water pours from a fountain. It ripples and spills over, and races off this way and that – always working overtime, picking up endless signals from the people it encounters, their thoughts, emotions, dreams and ideals. All is grist to the Aquarian mill. Original, inquisitive and charming, a typical Aquarian will make friends anywhere, anytime – in fact, they usually make several just by taking a walk around the block! They rather enjoy being different. And, in fact, 'being different' is something that comes naturally to Aquarius – as do the qualities of being kind and always ready to listen to those in need. If there is somebody you really like and yet don't quite know why, the chances are you've met an Aquarius.

Ruling Planet

Aquarius is traditionally ruled by Saturn, but modern astrologers – probably quite rightly – also give this sign to the more recently discovered Uranus, the planet of revolution and eccentricity. Aquarius people often have great flair and originality.

Element

Many people find it a surprise, but Aquarius the Water Carrier is actually an Air sign. It is also Fixed in nature, making for a character that is very thoughtful and intuitive and knows its own mind. Air signs are usually good communicators, and Aquarius is certainly no exception.

Physical Characteristics

Aquarians tend towards slow movements with a rather dreamy look to the features, as if deep in thought, which they usually are. There is sometimes a drooping head, from which they look upwards.

Health

Traditionally, Aquarius rules the ankles and lower legs, and weakness or damage to these areas can occur during falls. Sensitive and sometimes highly strung, Aquarians can suffer from mood swings, allergic reactions or unusual circulatory complaints – cramps, for example.

Famous Aquarians

Lord Byron
(Poet, born 22 January 1788)

Humphrey Bogart
(Actor, born 23 January 1899)

Oprah Winfrey
(Talk-show hostess, born 29 January 1954)

Charlotte Rampling
(Actress, born 5 February 1946)

Ronald Reagan
(US President, born 6 February 1911)

Charles Dickens
(Author, born 7 February 1812)

Mia Farrow
(Actress, born 9 February 1945)

Abraham Lincoln
(US President, born 12 February 1809)

Lucky Connections

Gemstones	Colours	Plants	Metals
sapphire	black	daffodil	aluminium
aquamarine	yellow	willow	lead
opal	fluorescent colours	pine	uranium
		hellebore	

Raising an **Aquarius** Child

Now listen carefully. Your Aquarius child is speaking, and you may think you know what they are talking about because the sentence began on a certain subject – but then suddenly there is a different subject, and another. And before the sentence is through, the subject has changed again! The Aquarian mind follows the beat of its own drum, and the flow of thoughts is so rapid and the connections and changes of direction so numerous that it is quite an achievement if you can keep up. This is the great quality of Aquarius, of course: its originality and inventiveness. If you live with an Aquarian you will almost be able to see the energetic sparks of invention flying. They are great listeners, too, because they are passionately interested in people and what makes them tick. As teenagers, the telephone may seem glued to the side of their heads at times, and your bills will be correspondingly astronomical. Easily distracted, their main difficulty lies in focusing and concentrating, and this is where parents can be helpful – in channelling this incredible energy constructively.

Aquarius in the family home

Aquarius children are extremely sensitive and intuitive. On the surface they may appear to be occupied and busy, but their in-built intuitive radar is tuned in to everything around them. They pick up on unspoken tensions around the home, and arguments and discord – expressed or unexpressed – can upset them deeply. Although there will always be rare moments when they simply insist on solitude, Aquarians usually love having visitors. They tend to get on best with their fellow Air signs, Libra and Gemini, but also quite well with Sagittarius and Aries.

Friendship

Friendship is what makes the Aquarius world go round, so there will always be someone on the other end of the line, or just around the corner to visit. All this can lead them towards a profound sense of humanity and love of their fellow men and women – or it can be an excuse for endless gossip and curiosity. Either way, Aquarians handle people who are anxious or upset very skilfully, and usually become *the* shoulder to cry on. These are the up-and-coming agony aunts (and uncles) of the zodiac.

School

At school, the Aquarius child might try to take the path of least resistance if allowed to, and this can quickly lead to under-achievement. Teachers might complain of their Aquarius pupils staring out of the window or not paying attention in class. They are thinking of so many things, of course – but does it get those exam passes at the end of the year? Probably not. Aquarians therefore have to learn the importance of concentration first of all, after which this same wayward, wandering mind will transform itself into one of the cleverest and most successful in the class.

Hobbies and interests

Aquarius children are independent little souls, and can quickly become rebellious. There is a fascination with everything that is new. They will sally forth on flashy bikes and scooters, mobile phone in hand, and later chill out on noisy computer games while listening to their favourite CDs. If guided away from all these distractions, however, they can become excellent artists or musicians with great flair and originality. Above all, Aquarians like people.

Choosing a Name for **Aquarius**

When seeking a name for Aquarius we can be as modern as we like, because of all the star signs this is arguably the one with the greatest fondness for new things, and for unusual ideas as well. There are many new names in our language that cannot be traced back by scholars to any one traditional source, and some of these naturally find their place here under Aquarius. Chelsea, a new and popular name ever since the Swinging Sixties in London, is a good example. Some say it means 'landing place', but for most of us it has a flamboyant association with fashion, popular culture and flair. This is a far more acceptable interpretation for modern names of this kind. Meanwhile, the love of the modern life can be seen in some unusual names such as Palmeda, meaning 'inventive', or Electra, 'brilliant', for the girls; and Fulbert, 'bright, shining', or even an old favourite, Neville, 'of the new city', for the boys.

In the English language there are numerous names signifying 'friend' and any of these can safely be entered in our lists of suitable names for Aquarius. These include the ever-popular David, 'beloved friend', and his many derivatives including Dai, Dafydd and the feminine derivatives Davina and Davinia. There are also some unusual alternatives, namely Sherwin, 'true friend', for the boys, and the delightful Amy, 'beloved', or Amice, 'friendship', for the girls. The famous Aquarian ability for counselling and advising others, particularly those who are disturbed or distressed, finds a resonance in names such as Monica, 'advisor', or Alfred, 'counsellor'.

Sometimes quite revolutionary in its ways, Aquarius is usually concerned with liberty and individuality. It is perhaps no accident, therefore, that its ruling planet, Uranus, was discovered in the late 18th century around the time of the great revolutions in France and America. Consequently, our lists include Charles and Carl, meaning 'free man', and the feminine derivatives Charlotte and Carla. From these popular names come some charming modern derivatives as well, especially for the girls, such as Charlene or Charlie. In Greek mythology, meanwhile, Uranus – referred to as 'the sky crowned with stars' – gives rise to several names that refer to stars, including Sterling, 'little star', or Celia, 'starry sky'.

The baptism of Christ, during which John the Baptist poured waters from the river Jordan above the head of Jesus, is one of the most enduring stories within the Christian tradition and is clearly applicable here to the sign of the Water Carrier. For this reason, John and the feminine Jane, Jean or Joan certainly find a place here, along with their many derivatives including Jonathan, Ivan and Ian for the boys, and Janet and Joanna for the girls. For similar reasons, the names Christian and Chris for the boys and Christiana and Kirsty for the girls have also been included in our lists.

At the baptism, a dove – symbol of the holy spirit – appeared over the head of Christ, so you will find names in our lists referring to the dove, or to any bird with mystical connotations. These include Jemima, 'dove', for the girls and Dovel, 'young dove', for the boys – and not forgetting the masculine Jordan itself, an excellent name for the Water Carrier.

100 Names for **Aquarius** Girls

A

Adiel ornament of the Lord
Agatha good
Allegra comforter, cheerful
Alma kind, loving, spirit mind
Althea truth
Amice friendship
Amity alternative form of Amice
Amy beloved
Ariadne delight, inventive
Arlene alternative form of Charleen
Astra star-like
Ava/Avis bird

C

Caelia heavenly, starry sky
Candace/Candice glowing
Cara friend, beloved
Carla/Karla/Carly/Charlie alternative forms of Caroline
Carleen alternative form of Caroline
Carol/Carole alternative forms of Caroline
Caroline/Carrie free
Celesta/Celestina/Celestine alternative forms of Celeste
Celeste heavenly, starry sky
Celia starry sky
Centella flashing light
Charity caring, kind
Charlene/Charleen/Sharleen alternative forms of Caroline
Charlotte alternative form of Caroline
Charmain/Charmaine songful, delight
Chelsea landing place, fashion
Chimalis bluebird
Chiquita little one
Chispa spark
Christabel beautiful Christian

Christabella/Christabelle alternative forms of Christabel
Christiana Christian
Christie alternative form of Christiana
Christina/Krystyna alternative forms of Christiana
Christine alternative form of Christiana
Colinette young dove
Columbia dove
Columbine dove
Consuela one who consoles
Corolla small crown
Crystal crystal, many-faceted
Cyane deep blue

D

Davida/Davina/Davinia beloved friend
Dema arbiter
Dova dove
Dusty modern usage

E

Electra brilliant
Elvia of keen mind
Elvina wise, friendly
Emma whole, universal
Essie alternative form of Estalla
Estalla/Estera star
Ethelwyn noble friend

F

Frances free

G

Gill/Gilly/Jill diminutives of Gillian
Gillian servant of St John
Gudrid divine impulse

Friendly Intuitive Inventive

H

Hebe cup bearer to the gods, youthful

I

Imogen visionary, imaginative

J

Jane baptism, grace of God
Janet little Jane, little one of divine grace
Janice alternative form of Jane
Janine/Janelle alternative forms of Jane
Jean/Jeanette alternative forms of Jane
Jemima dove
Joan alternative form of Jane
Joanna/Joanne alternative forms of Jane

K

Kelda spring or fountain
Kirstie/Kirsty alternative forms of Christiana
Kristen/Kristin alternative forms of Christiana

L

Leila/Leilah dark-haired, swarthy
Lyn/Lynn refreshing, water pool, pretty
Lynna cascade
Lyris musical, song of the lyre
Lysandra liberator

M

Melina gentle
Melody singer of songs
Monica adviser
Morag great young one

N

Novia new

O

Opal gemstone (of Aquarius)
Ophelia helper
Ophrah/Oprah fawn
Orella she who listens

P

Palmeda inventive
Paloma dove
Pandora universal gift, all-gifted
Penelope duck
Penny diminutive of Penelope

R

Ruth vision, compassion, friend

S

Sharon to sing (also the plain)
Sian alternative form of Jane
Sky sky

U

Undine water sprite
Urbana polite, urban woman

V

Vera truth, faith
Veronica true image, compassion

100 Names for **Aquarius** Boys

A

Ainsley one meadow, his own self
Aldwin old friend
Alfred counsellor
Alpheus god of the river
Alvin elfin friend
Ambrose immortal
Angus unique choice
Auberon alternative form of Aubrey
Aubrey elf-power, supernaturally
Aylwin devoted friend

B

Baptista/Batista/Battista baptized
Bertwin illustrious friend
Boniface doer of good, benefactor
Bromwell dweller by wild broom spring
Byrle cup bearer

C

Callum/Calum dove
Carl/Karl alternative forms of Charles
Chae/Chas/Chaz/Chuck diminutives of Charles
Charles/Charlie free man
Charlton alternative form of Charles
Chris diminutive of Christopher and Christian
Christian Christian
Christopher bearer of Christ
Christy/Christoph alternative forms of Christopher
Clive riverbank
Clyde river, washer
Colin dove, young chieftain
Colvin dark friend

D

Dafydd alternative form of David
Dai alternative form of David
Dave/Davey diminutives of David
David beloved friend
Declan full of goodness
Derwin valued friend of the people
Dilwyn calm friend
Dovel young dove
Drew manly, skilled in magic

E

Eaton from the riverside
Ebert of active mind
Edwin good friend or ally
Eldred mature counsellor
Eldwin old friend
Elford dweller by the ford
Elvan quick-willed
Erastus amiable
Erwin friend

F

Farquhar friendly man
Fergus man of vigour
Findal inventive
Francis free
Franklin/Franklyn free man
Frewen free friend
Fulbert bright, shining

G

Godwin good friend, God's friend
Granville from the big town

Friendly Intuitive **Inventive**

H

Hadwin family friend
Harvey progressive, battle ready
Heilyn cup bearer
Herbert man of brilliance
Hubert bright mind, bright spirit

I

Ian alternative form of John
Ivan alternative form of John

J

John baptism, grace of God
Jonah/Jonas dove
Jonathan alternative form of John
Jordan flowing down, place of baptism
Jovita little dove

K

Kelsey from the water
Kendall spring water
Kirby water skin
Kit diminutive of Christopher

L

Linford ford by the linden
Lubin beloved friend
Lyndell dweller by the cascade

M

Malcolm devotee of the dove
Marvin famous friend

N

Neville of the new city
Newton of the new town

O

Orban citizen
Orel listener

P

Philander he who loves mankind

Q

Quinn counsel

R

Rodney reed island

S

Sandford sandy ford or crossing
Saul asked for
Sean/Shane/Shaun/Shawn alternative forms of John
Sherwin true friend
Stanford stony crossing
Sterling/Stirling little star

T

Taliesin shining brow
Thomas doubt, twin

U

Urban of the town
Urlwin noble friend

W

Winslow from the friendly hill
Winston dweller in a friendly town
Winthrop from the friendly village
Woodrow/Woody houses by the wood, popular

X

Xavier new house

Z

Zachary God has remembered

Pisces

♓ (The Fishes)

20 February to **20 March**

Pisces is usually represented by two fish, bound together but swimming in opposite directions, and this will sound familiar to you if you have a Piscean baby or child. They swim dreamily through life, this way and that, sometimes upwards towards the light, at others down into the mysterious depths. Peaceable, sensitive, poetic, modest – these are all features of the Piscean personality that endear them to their fellows. But it isn't always easy to understand their routine, or lack of one: Pisceans of any age can sleep all day and stay awake all night, and it will seem perfectly natural to them. They have their own rhythm and their own unique priorities which do not necessarily concur with those of our busy, materialistic society. They live life very much in the slow lane and usually love every minute of it, savouring to the full all the many delights along the way.

Ruling Planet

Traditionally, Pisces is ruled by Jupiter, but modern astrologers also give it to the more recently discovered Neptune. This is a good choice, since Neptune is a mystical, intuitive planet with many hidden dimensions. It brings additional qualities of inspiration to the already naturally artistic Piscean personality.

Element

Pisces is a Water element and is Mutable in nature – a very elusive combination which is hard to classify. Fishes are slippery, and so are Pisceans – mysterious, inscrutable and often swimming contrary to the prevailing trend.

Physical Characteristics

Sometimes rather delicate and slender in appearance, Pisces people have a certain daintiness or finesse about them. The limbs are sometimes short, especially below the knee, and they often appear to be conscious of their feet, looking down frequently or stepping carefully.

Health

Traditionally, Pisces rules the feet – suggesting weakness or disorders here and in the lower limbs – bunions or oedema, for example. The personality can crave stimulation, occasionally leading to over-indulgence or addictive behaviour.

Famous Pisceans

Cindy Crawford
(Model, born 20 February 1966)

Zeppo Marx
(Comic actor, born 25 February 1901)

Elizabeth Taylor
(Actress, born 27 February 1932)

David Niven
(Actor, born 1 March 1910)

Glenn Miller
(Band leader, born 1 March 1904)

Sharon Stone
(Actress, born 10 March 1958)

Liza Minnelli
(Singer and actress, born 12 March 1946)

Albert Einstein
(Mathematician, born 14 March 1879)

Lucky Connections

Gemstones	Colours	Plants	Metal
emerald	green	betony	tin
coral	coral	willowherb	
chrysolite	navy blue	water lily	
jade		poppy	

Raising a **Pisces** Child

Tread softly – otherwise you may be treading on your little Pisces' dreams. Pisceans are the natural poets of the zodiac and their deep urge towards self-expression does battle daily with the contrary flow of shyness and modesty. Don't worry if your bubbly little Piscean suddenly becomes sulky and aloof – those silent, moody phases are just moments of essential introspection, and their privacy has to be respected at such times. By the same token, harsh words or brutality will wound them deeply. Remember the fishes – you have to handle them delicately, otherwise you will rub off all those sensitive scales. Be prepared for tearful moments when this happens, but also for forgiveness – a quality which Pisceans respect greatly in others and are able to summon up themselves very easily and naturally. As they grow and learn, and provided they can be guarded from the coarseness and temptation of their more cynical cousins, the fishes can swim upwards to the light, confidently, and become people of great compassion and goodness.

Pisces in the family home

Schedules and routines are not high on the list of priorities for Pisces children, and they will instead prefer an environment in which they can play freely and express their own vivid imagination in creative pursuits. They will love painting, play-acting and conjuring up all manner of curious fantasies. There may well be fairies at the bottom of a Piscean's garden – and remember, their fantasy world is real to them. They get on best with their fellow Water signs, Scorpio and Cancer, but also quite well with Taurus and Capricorn.

Friendship

Your Pisces child will enjoy people who are different, a little more laid back or cool than most. Although content to play indoors, they do not like being confined in one place for too long, and so friends have to be adaptable, to join in with the theatrical, creative world they build around themselves and to accept the fact that the games themselves have no rules or regulations. For the same reason, Pisceans do not take kindly to bossy children or bullies.

School

Somewhat disinterested in worldly ambition, the dreamy, easy-going Piscean needs quite a bit of encouragement and even a little coercion at times to get started at school, otherwise apathy and a certain cynicism can quickly set in. Given suitable exposure and good teachers, however, subjects at which Pisceans can excel are literature, poetry, art, design, dance and music. Soccer is the ideal sport for this sign that traditionally rules the feet. So perhaps there is a way to make your little Piscean get some fresh air, after all!

Hobbies and interests

You won't find too many Pisces children taking up building or engineering for a hobby. Rather, look for the dreamy fishes in off-beat, artistic circles. Concerts, dancing, cool parties or hanging out are more to their liking than groups or associations with stuffy rules to abide by. They can be attracted to those living on the fringe of society – from either a philanthropic mission, or a desire to drop out and turn on. Parents who are vigilant can play a major role in helping these idealistic little fishes to swim in the right direction.

Choosing a Name for **Pisces**

Little Pisceans will relate to names that reflect their thoughtful, intuitive minds and the sense of wonder and devotion they often feel inside. Suitable names include the popular favourite Ann, meaning simply 'grace', or Gregory, 'vigilant', and the more unusual Imogen, 'visionary', or Clement, 'merciful'. Meanwhile, the delicate Pisces character (and sometimes their slender, petite shape as well) finds quite a persuasive resonance in the mischievous figures of elves or fairies – the 'little people' found in so many folk traditions the world over. Some unusual names like Alvina, 'elfin friend', or Elra, 'elfin wisdom', can be chosen for the girls, along with the more modern and popular Kayleigh, meaning 'slender'. For the boys, there is the ever-popular Paul, which means 'small, humble, modest', or the more exotic Rhonwen for the girls, from the Welsh word for 'slender and fair'.

But of course Pisces is also a Water sign, ruled by Neptune, the great god of the sea in ancient mythology. Many cultures have a vigorous tradition of brave seamen and explorers, and for the boys particularly we have numerous Gaelic or Celtic names referring to seamen or sea warriors beginning with the letter M. These include Morgan, 'sea born', Mortimer or Murphy, both meaning 'sea warrior', or the rugged seamen Morven, Murdoch and Murray. The girls, meanwhile, have some beautiful sea names including Guinevere, 'white wave', from which we derive the more popular Jennifer and Jenny, or the delightful Nerissa, meaning 'sea nymph'.

Pisces always remains the great mystical sign of the zodiac, and perhaps the most self-expressive and penetrating of all. It is also a sign which, from very early times, became associated with the birth of Christianity. A symbol depicting a fish was used as a secret sign of recognition among early Christians while Jesus made his disciples, the poor men of Galilee, 'fishers of men'. Names taken from this story such as Peter – the fisherman who became the 'rock' on which the Church and its religion were built – or Christiana and Christian are all worthy choices.

In earlier cultures there were several powerful mythological gods whose characteristics were absorbed into Christianity. These include the god of wine, Dionysus: Jesus compared himself to the vine, and for practising Christians he remains to this day the saviour who gave his blood – still represented by wine in the holy communion or mass. Names derived from Dionysus are therefore significant in our list and include Dion or the more traditional Dennis for the boys, plus their feminine counterparts, Dionne or Denise, for the girls.

With the combination of Jupiter and Neptune as ruling bodies, there is at the heart of many a Piscean soul an enduring combination of benevolence, humility and self-sacrifice. Nowhere is this illustrated better than in the story of Cinderella, one of the most widespread of all folk stories and from which we derive the modern name Cindy. This great quality of humility is also illustrated powerfully in the biblical account of Mary Magdalene, who washed Christ's feet and dried them with her hair, so we have names such as Madeleine, derivatives Madge and Maddie, and of course Mary herself. Suitable names for the boys in this context would be Miles, 'mild, merciful warrior', or Samuel, 'heard of God'. Still with feet, and perhaps on a lighter note, we also have names like Olwin, meaning 'white footprint', Agrippina, 'born feet first', and Rigel, the name of a star in the constellation of Orion but also an Arabic word meaning 'foot'.

100 Names for **Pisces** Girls

A

Agrippina born feet first
Aislin/Aisling/Ashling dream, vision
Alana my child
Alvina elfin friend
Ann grace
Annabel/Annabella/Annabelle beautiful Ann

B

Bassania of the deep-sea realm

C

Caitlin/Caitlyn alternative forms of Katherine
Carmel vineyard or garden
Cattima slender reed
Charity benevolent, charitable
Christabel beautiful Christian
Christabella/Christabelle alternative forms of Christabel
Christiana Christian
Christie alternative form of Christiana
Christina/Krystyna alternative forms of Christiana
Cinderella humble, little cinder
Cindy alternative form of Cinderella
Clementina/Clementine merciful, gentle
Coreen/Corinna/Corinne maiden, girl
Cressa from watercress
Cyrene river nymph

D

Damaris gentle
Delinda gentle
Denise from Dionysus, god of wine
Dione/Dionne alternative form of Denise
Donella little maid
Dulcibella/Dulcie/Dulcy sweet

E

Elra elfin wisdom
Elva elfin
Emerald precious stone (of Jupiter)
Emogene alternative form of Imogen
Erlina little elf
Evangeline/Evangelina of the gospel

F

Fabrianne maid of good works
Fay faith, fairy

G

Gilda servant of God, gilded
Glenda holy and good
Glenis/Glenys good, pure
Grace grace
Gracia/Gracie/Gratia alternative forms of Grace
Graine/Grania affectionate, love
Guinevere/Gwinny white wave, fair wife

H

Hala halo
Halcyon calm, of the sea

I

Immy/Imogena/Imogene alternative forms of Imogen
Imogen visionary, beloved child

J

Jade semi-precious stone (of Jupiter)
Jennifer alternative form of Guinevere
Jenny diminutive of Jennifer
Julia/Juliana soft-haired, downy
Juliet alternative form of Julia

K

Kachina sacred dance
Karen/Karena/Karin/Karina alternative forms of Katherine
Kate/Katie/Kitty diminutives of Katherine
Katherine/Catherine/Katharine/Kathryn pure, self-sacrifice
Kathleen beautiful eyes
Katinka alternative form of Katherine
Katrine alternative form of Katherine
Kayley/Kayleigh/Caileigh/Caleigh slender
Kirsten/Kirstie/Kirsty alternative forms of Christiana
Kolina pure
Kristen/Kristin alternative forms of Christiana

L

Linda pretty, neat
Lydia woman of Lydia, baptized
Lynn alternative form of Linda

M

Maddie/Madge/Magda diminutives of Magdalene
Madeleine/Magdalen alternative forms of Magdalene
Madlin/Madlyn/Madoline alternative forms of Magdalene
Maeve intoxication
Magdalene woman of Magdala, Mary Magdalene
Maria/Marie alternative forms of Mary
Marian/Marion alternative forms of Mary
Marilyn/Marylyn of Mary's line
Marina maiden of the sea
Mary wished-for child, the Magdalene
Mena mercy
Mercy compassion, mercy
Meryl/Muriel sea bright, fragrant myrrh
Mollie/Molly diminutives of Mary

N

Nancy/Nanette alternative forms of Ann
Nanine dainty little maid
Nata dancer
Nerissa sea nymph

O

Olwen/Olwin/Olwyn white footprint
Ondine alternative form of Undine

P

Pamela all sweetness, gift of the elf
Paula alternative form of Pauline
Paulette alternative form of Pauline
Pauline/Paulina little one
Petra/Petrina/Petrona rock
Poppy flower (of Neptune)

R

Reva dreamer
Rhonwen alternative form of Rowena
Rigel foot
Ronnie diminutive of Rowena
Rowena/Rowina slender, fair, joyful
Ruella lucky elfin one

S

Sancha/Sanchia holy
Sida water lily

T

Thelma wish

U

Undine water sprite

100 Names for **Pisces** Boys

A
Admetus untamed
Adriel of God's flock
Arlin sea bound

B
Bainbridge of the sea
Baldric warrior's sash or belt
Blaine bubble

C
Carew castle near the water
Carrick rocky headland
Chip diminutive of Christopher
Chris diminutive of Christian or Christopher
Christian Christian
Christoph/Krystof alternative forms of Christopher
Christopher/Kristoffer bearer of Christ
Christy diminutive of Christopher
Clement merciful, mild
Cordell cord

D
Darius preserver
Denis/Dennis from Dionysus, god of wine
Denny/Denys/Denzil alternative forms of Denis
Devlin pilgrim
Dewar pilgrim
Dion alternative form of Denis
Dwight alternative form of Denis
Dylan sea, poetic

E
Edsel rich in self
Eldo wish
Elika purified by God
Enold anointed
Evar life

F
Fairburn comely child
Finnegan fair

G
Gareth gentle
Gary alternative form of Gareth
Gersham/Gershom exiled
Godfrey peace of God
Goodard pious, resolute
Greg/Gregg alternative forms of Gregory
Gregor alternative form of Gregory
Gregory vigilant
Gurth bonded
Gwion elf

I
Irfon anointed one
Isa equal
Ishmael God heareth

J
Jeremiah exalted of God
Jeremy/Jerry diminutives of Jeremiah
Joachim may God exalt
Jules diminutive of Julian
Julian soft-haired, of downy beard

K
Kelsey from the water
Kelwin dweller by the water
Kit diminutive of Christopher

L
Lachlan by the sea, inlet
Lee poem, clearing in a wood
Linden alternative form of Linford
Linford/Linfred of gentle grace

M
Matthew/Matthias gift of God
Meade strong draught
Mergus diver
Merton from or near the sea
Miles/Myles mild, merciful warrior
Morgan sea born, seaman
Mortimer sea warrior
Morven seaman
Moses drawn from the waters
Murdoch/Murdock seaman
Murphy sea warrior
Murray seaman

N
Nathan alternative form of Nathanial
Nathaniel/Nathanael God has given
Nevlin seaman, sailor
Noam pleasant, delight

O
Ola eternity

P
Palmer pilgrim
Paul/Pawley small, humble, modest
Pearce/Pierce/Piers alternative forms of Peter
Peter rock, disciple, fisherman
Pierre alternative form of Peter

R
Remus fair
Renauld reborn
Romeo pilgrim to Rome, romantic
Romero wanderer
Roscoe sea horse

S
Salvador/Salvatore saviour
Sam/Sammy diminutives of Samuel
Samuel heard of God
Sancho holy
Saul asked of God
Seadon/Seaton dweller by the sea
Selmar rolling sea
Seth appointed
Seward warden of the sea coast
Sherwood sea ruler
Stig wanderer

T
Tristram sorrowful

V
Vaughan little, modest

Z
Zac/Zach/Zack/Zak diminutives of Zacharias
Zacharias remembered of the Lord
Zachary alternative form of Zacharias
Zurial God is my rock

Compatibility Charts

The following charts – one for each star sign – show those signs which are most compatible with one another in astrological terms. This classification is based upon the common ground shared between signs belonging to the same element. For example: Aries, being a Fire sign, gets on best with Leo and Sagittarius, the other two Fire signs of the zodiac. If you view the zodiac as a circle, as is usually done in astrological charts, this relationship forms a triangle, a 120 degree separation, called a Trine. The Trine draws together signs of the same element, which are considered harmonious in nature and mutually supportive.

In addition, signs with half this separation – that is, at a 60 degree angle – are also reasonably compatible. Sticking with the example of Aries, this means that this sign also gets on quite well with Aquarius and Gemini. The relationship is not quite as strong as with Leo and Sagittarius, but is still good enough.

Of course, human nature is a complex business and this is only a very simple way of estimating compatibility – even in a purely astrological sense, it is very basic. The stars 'incline', they do not 'compel'. Nevertheless, charts of this kind are still worth considering and sometimes offer some very useful insights into how people react to one another within the home or family group.

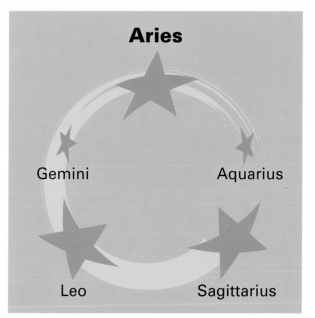

Aries

Gemini · Aquarius · Leo · Sagittarius

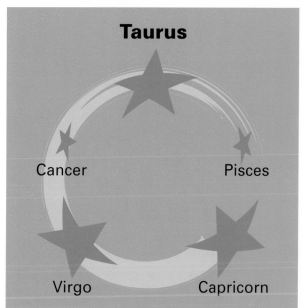

Taurus

Cancer · Pisces · Virgo · Capricorn

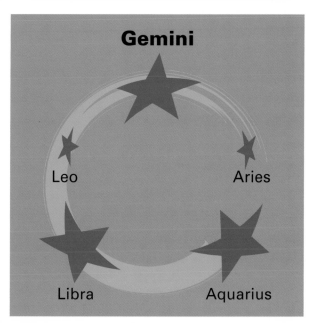

Gemini

Leo · Aries · Libra · Aquarius

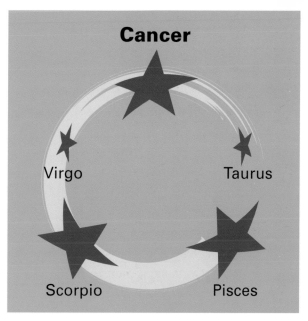

Cancer

Virgo · Taurus · Scorpio · Pisces

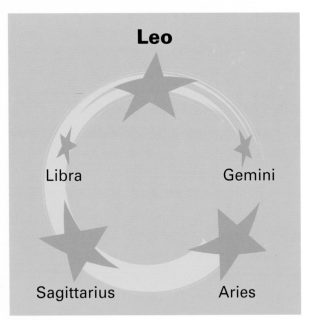

Leo

Libra · Gemini · Sagittarius · Aries

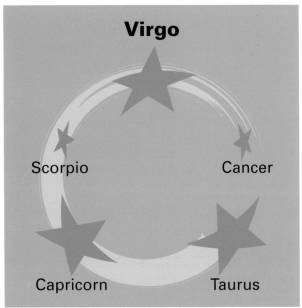

Virgo

Scorpio · Cancer · Capricorn · Taurus

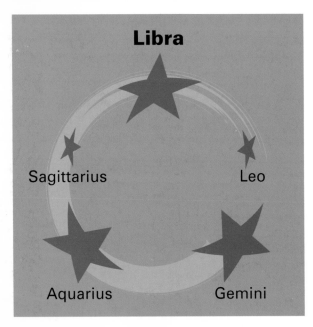

Libra

Sagittarius · Leo · Aquarius · Gemini

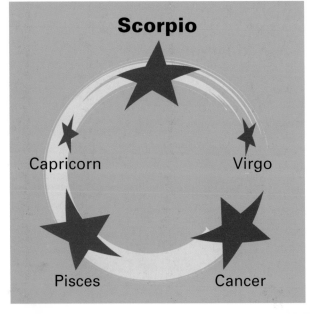

Scorpio

Capricorn · Virgo · Pisces · Cancer

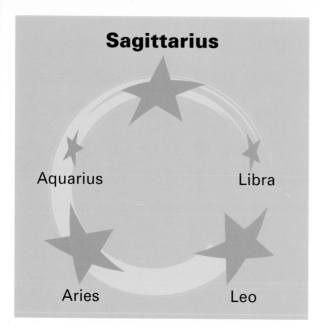

Sagittarius

Aquarius · Libra · Aries · Leo

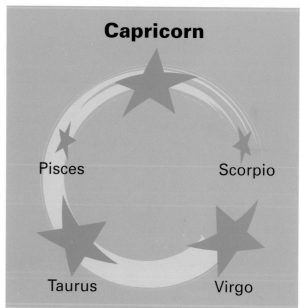

Capricorn

Pisces · Scorpio · Taurus · Virgo

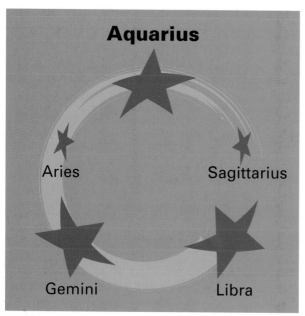

Aquarius

Aries · Sagittarius · Gemini · Libra

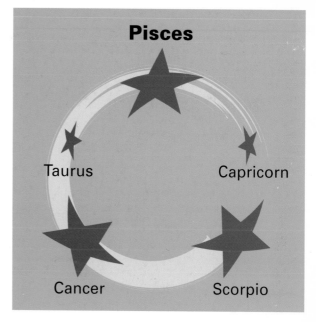

Pisces

Taurus · Capricorn · Cancer · Scorpio

And finally

If you want to find out more about astrology or would like to contact a professionally qualified astrologer who will be able to draw up and interpret a full natal chart for you, go to www.starnames.fsnet.co.uk, where you will find up-to-date news and information to help you.

Acknowledgements

Executive Editor **Jane McIntosh**

Editor **Sharon Ashman**

Senior Designer **Rozelle Bentheim**

Design and artwork **Burville-Riley**

Production Controller **Lucy Woodhead**